KB275960

Great-Grandpa's in the Litter Box

Great-Grandpa's in the Litter Box

by Dan Greenburg
Illustrated by Jack E. Davis

I'd like to thank my editors,
Jane O'Connor and Judy Donnelly,
who make the process of writing and revising
so much fun, and without whom
these books would not exist.

I also want to thank
Jennifer Dussling and Laura Driscoll
for their terrific ideas.

For Judith, and for the real Zack,

with love—D.G.

My name is Zack. I'm ten years old and I guess you could say I've been interested in **weird stuff** all my life. Stuff like **haunt**ed houses, UFOs,[1] and **storm**s where it rains frogs. So when something weird happened to me, I was probably more **open-minded**

---

1 **UFO** (= Unidentified Flying Object) 미확인 비행물체. 전문가의 눈이나 전파 탐지 등으로도 정체를 탐지할 수 없는 비행체를 말한다.

than somebody else who wasn't interested in weird stuff all their life.

I was in the animal **shelter** near our home in New York City. After years of **beg**ging my dad for a cat, he finally **broke down** and said yes. I could get a **kitten**. So here I was.

I passed a **cage** with an old gray **tomcat** inside it. His **fur** was **matted** with **dirt**. He'd lost half the **whisker**s on the left side of his face, which made him look a little **lopsided**. And the **tip** had been **chew**ed off of one of his ears.

"Sssst! Young man!" Someone was calling me. The voice sounded **raspy** and strange. "Hello, little boy! Over here!"

I turned around, looking to see who it

was. But there was nobody in **sight**.

I went on to a cage where a little tuxedo[2] kitten with a black body and white **paw**s was taking a **nap**. He sure was cute. I stopped to take a closer look at him. Of course, it probably wasn't the best time for me to **adopt** a kitten. In a couple of days my dad and I were flying to Chicago to spend Thanksgiving[3] with my Grandma Leah. But our **neighbor** had agreed to cat-sit.[4] And I wasn't **taking** any **chance**s of my dad changing his mind.

I'd almost decided on that cute little

2　**tuxedo** 마치 턱시도 코트를 입은 것처럼 하얀색과 검은색이 섞인 털을 지닌 고양이를 가리키는 표현.

3　**Thanksgiving** 추수감사절. 북미 지역의 전통적 명절이자 국경일로 이 날 칠면조 구이를 먹는 풍습이 있다.

4　**cat-sit** 'baby-sit(아기를 봐 주다)'라는 말에 'baby' 대신 'cat'을 넣어서 사용한 표현으로 '고양이를 봐 주다'라는 뜻이다.

tuxedo kitten when I heard the voice again:

"Hey, kid," said the voice. "I am *speaking* to you."

"Where are you?" I asked.

"Right here, **dummy**," said the voice. "In the cage in back of you."

I turned around. That **scruffy** old gray tomcat was **staring** quite **cross**ly at me.

"You'll **pardon** me for **holler**ing," said the cat. "But I was afraid you **were about to** make a terrible mistake and choose somebody else."

"You can *talk!*" I said, **hardly** able to **believe my ears**.

I moved closer to his cage. I wanted to see if his cat **lip**s moved when he talked.

Maybe this was just a **trick**—somebody doing ventriloquism.[5] I mean I told you I like weird stuff, but this was really **far out**, even for me. "A talking cat?" I said.

"Yeah, a talking cat, how about that," said the cat **sarcastic**ally.

His cat lips were moving! This was no trick!

"But look at you—a talking boy," he said. "Listen, we don't have much time. You've got to get me out of here."

"What do you mean?"

"I mean I can't **stand** it in here a minute longer," he said. "The **meow**ing and the smell are **driving** me right **up the wall**.

---

5 **ventriloquism** 복화술. 입을 움직이지 않고 말하는 기술. 주로 인형을 가지고 공연을 할 때, 인형이 말하는 것처럼 보이게 하는 데 사용한다.

Tell them you're adopting me."

"Uh, I don't mean to hurt your feelings," I said. "But I've already decided on this little tuxedo kitten here." Like I said before, I'm pretty open-minded. I had nothing against talking cats. I just wasn't sure I wanted to live with one. Especially with one as **bossy** as this one seemed.

"The tuxedo kitten?" he said. "Poor choice."

"What do you mean?"

"He has **flea**s and **worm**s. Plus he never **got the hang of** using a **litter** box."

The tomcat gave me a long look. He could see I wasn't **buy**ing it.

"OK," the cat **went on**. "I didn't want to have to use this. But here goes: If you don't adopt me, they're going to **put** me **to sleep**. And I don't mean **tuck** me in bed in my **jammies** either. I mean kill me. You really want that on your **conscience**, kid?"

"Listen, they don't put cats to sleep here," I said. "That is a **well-known** fact." This cat was not only bossy, he also seemed to have problems with the truth.

"OK, I **admit** they haven't lately," he said. "But that could change any day."

I looked at him and shook my head.

"OK, OK," he said. "How's about this: What if I told you I know your name?"

"What's my name?"

"Zack."

"How—how did you know that?" I asked. I had to admit I was pretty

impressed. Not that many people know my name, and even fewer cats.

"You're impressed, huh?" said the big gray tomcat. "What if I told you I'm a member of your family, Zack? Do you think you'd still prefer the little tuxedo?"

"A member of my *family*?" I said. "How could that be? You're a cat."

"Hey, you never heard of **reincarnation**? Somebody dies and comes back as somebody else?"

"So?" I said. Sure, I'd heard of reincarnation. In fact, I'd read about several cases in India of kids who **claim**ed to have lived before. They knew facts about certain places they'd never been, things they couldn't possibly have known if they were **ordinary** kids. Still, they were kids, not cats. "So what?"

"So," said the gray tomcat, "I happen to be your wonderful dead Great-Grandfather Julius."

Chapter 2

One minute I'm **about to** go home with a cute little black-and-white **kitten**, the next a big gray **tomcat** tells me he's my dead great-grandfather. I didn't know what to do. I took another look at the kitten. He was **lick**ing his front **paw** in an **adorable** way. The tomcat saw I was still **lean**ing **toward** the kitten.

"What? You don't think I'm cute?" he asked. Then he **pose**d in what he must have thought was a cute pose.

"You're . . . *kind* of cute, sir," I said. "It's just that . . ."

"Cute, shmute,[1]" he said. "You can't tell me you're going to walk out of here with a **flea-bitten** stranger who hasn't been **proper**ly **toilet-train**ed and leave your **beloved** great-grandfather **rot**ting in a **stink**ing little **cage**? Family is family, Zack."

I looked at the tomcat, then at the kitten, then at the tomcat. *Family is family.* Funny, that's something Grandma Leah always

---

1 **shm-** 접두사로 단어의 앞에 붙여 무시하거나 경멸하는 뜻이 담긴 표현을 만들 수 있다.

says. That did it.

"I guess you're right, sir," I said. "I guess family is family."

"Now you're **talk**ing **sense**, kid," said the cat. "And, please, call me Great-Grandpa Julius."

When I arrived home, **huff**ing **and puff**ing, carrying my cardboard[1] cat **carrier**, my dad met me at the door. Since my parents **split** up, I live part of the time with my dad and part with my mom.

"So," he said, smiling, "it looks like

---

1 **cardboard** 판지. 두껍고 단단하게 만든 종이.

you've finally gotten yourself a **kitty**."

"Yeah," I said, and put the cat carrier down. I was **exhaust**ed. With Great-Grandpa Julius inside it, it must have **weigh**ed close to thirty pounds.[2]

"Can I see the little guy?" asked my dad.

"Sure, Dad," I said. "But first I have to tell you a couple of things."

"OK, what?"

"Well, number one, I didn't get a kitten. I got a **slight**ly older cat."

"Why,[3] Zack," said my dad, "I think that's a wonderful thing to do, giving an

---

2 **pound** 무게의 단위 파운드. 1파운드는 약 0.45킬로그램이다. (30파운드 는 약 13.6킬로그램이다.)

3 **why** 여기에서는 이유를 묻거나 말할 때 쓰는 의문사 또는 관계사가 아닌 '어머', '아니'라는 뜻의 감탄사로 쓰였다.

older cat a home. I'm very proud of you, son."

"Uh-huh. And number two, he's not an **ordinary** cat, Dad. He's . . . well, for one thing, he talks."

"He talks," said my dad.

"Yeah, he talks."

My dad smiled, deciding to **go along with** my little **joke**.

"I see. Well, what does he say?"

"He says he's Great-Grandpa Julius."

"I didn't even think you remembered having a Great-Grandpa Julius," he said, **chuckling**.

What I remembered was hearing Grandma Leah **go on** about her father, Julius, who was so nice he was **practical**ly a **saint**. Then she'd always add how Julius was the complete **opposite** of Great-Grandpa Maurice, her husband's father. Maurice was the **black sheep** of the family.

So far, Julius didn't seem that saintly to me. I opened the cat carrier. Great-Grandpa Julius and my dad took a good long look at each other.

"Well, he's certainly . . . big," said my dad. "Hello, Great-Grandpa Julius. Remember me? Dan? You always used to say I was your favorite grandchild. Can you say hello?"

Great-Grandpa Julius seemed **about to** say something. Then he **scratch**ed behind his ear with his **hind** leg instead.

"He's not very **talkative**," said my dad.

"You should have heard him at the animal **shelter**," I said.

My dad chuckled and walked off, shaking his head.

"How come you didn't talk to my dad?" I asked.

"I talk when I want to," said the cat, "not when other people want me to. Hey, Zack, you got anything to eat around here? I'm so hungry I could eat **rodent**s."

I had the free can of cat food they gave me at the animal shelter. I put it into a **bowl** on the floor. Great-Grandpa Julius **sniff**ed it and **wrinkle**d up his nose.

"Feh!" he said. "What *is* that **stuff**?"

"Beef **by-product**s in gravy,[4]" I replied.

"You got maybe a little herring[5] with sour cream?[6]"

I told him we didn't have anything like that. He did not take this at all well.

"Let's put it this way, kid," said Great-Grandpa Julius. "Either get me some herring with sour cream **pronto**, or I'm going to take a **leak** on your sofa."

"You're not serious about this," I said.

"Try me," he said.

If you ask me, Great-Grandpa Julius was a lot **crankier** than I'd heard. But I was trying to be understanding. I guess dying

---

4 **gravy** 그레이비. 고기를 익힐 때 나온 육즙에 밀가루 등을 넣어 만든 소스.

5 **herring** 청어. 청어과의 바닷물고기로 등은 짙은 청색이고, 배는 은백색인 등 푸른 생선의 한 종류이다.

6 **sour cream** 사워크림. 생크림을 발효시켜 만든 새콤한 맛이 나는 크림.

and getting **reincarnate**d as a cat could **spoil** a person's **mood**.

Luckily, the **deli** on the corner sold herring with sour cream. I brought it back to Great-Grandpa Julius.

"Now you're talking,[1]" he said when he saw it. He **gobble**d it up. "Not bad. Not bad at all. But tomorrow, Zack, be sure

---

1 **now you are talking** 다른 사람이 하는 말에 동의하거나 찬성할 때 쓰는 표현으로 '바로 그거야!' 또는 '그거 좋은 생각이야!'라는 뜻이다.

the deli man doesn't **skimp** on the sour cream."

Boy,[2] this cat was **pushy**!

"Listen, I can't buy you herring and sour cream every day," I said. "I only get three dollars a week **allowance**. And I won't be able to buy it for you over Thanksgiving weekend—I won't even be here. I'm going to Chicago. To visit Grandma Leah."

"We're going to visit Leah?" he asked **delighted**ly.

"*I* am," I said. "You're staying here with a **neighbor**."

"You'd go to Chicago and you wouldn't take me to see my own daughter? If Leah

---

2 **boy** 여기에서는 '소년'이라는 뜻이 아니라, '맙소사!' 또는 '어머나!'라는 의미로 놀람이나 실망, 기쁨 등을 나타내는 표현으로 쓰였다.

heard I was reincarnated and didn't come to see her, she'd be **crush**ed."

"Well," I said, "let me ask my dad."

"Zack," said my dad, "I'm **willing** to **go along with** a **joke**. But we both know cats can't talk. Although I must **admit** I'm **tempt**ed to bring him to Chicago, just to see the expression on Grandma Leah's face when you tell her that cat is her father."

"Dad, I'd really like to take him to Chicago. I think it would mean a lot to him."

"I'll tell you what," said my dad. "If you can get him to talk to me, you can take him to Chicago."

I went back to my room, where Great-

Grandpa Julius was **paw**ing through my **collection** of baseball cards.

"You have any cards with Lou Gehrig,[3] Ty Cobb,[4] or Rogers Hornsby[5] on them?" he asked.

"No, I'm afraid not."

"Gehrig and Hornsby were nice **fella**s. Cobb not so nice."

"That's what I hear."

"But all three **sign**ed my baseball."

"You're saying you actually met Lou Gehrig, Ty Cobb, and Rogers Hornsby?" I

---

3 **Lou Gehrig** 루 게릭. 뉴욕 양키스(New York Yankees)팀에서 4번 타자로 활약한 미국의 프로 야구 선수. 근육 위축증으로 사망하여, 이 병에 그의 이름이 별명으로 붙었다.

4 **Ty Cobb** 타이 코브 또는 타이러스 코브(Tyrus Cobb). 디트로이트 타이거스(Detroit Tigers)팀에서 외야수로 활약한 미국의 프로 야구 선수.

5 **Rogers Hornsby** 로저스 혼즈비. 미국의 프로 야구 선수, 코치이자 감독. 메이저리그 역사상 가장 위대한 타자들 가운데 한 사람으로 손꼽힌다.

said. The **tomcat nod**ded. "What happened to the ball they signed?"

"I have it."

"Where?"

"In a safe place, don't worry about it. So did your dad say I could come to Chicago?"

"He said on one **condition**."

"What's that?"

"You have to talk to him. I don't think he believes you can talk."

"That's all I have to do, talk to him?"

"That's all."

"OK, let's do it."

I followed Great-Grandpa Julius, who **pad**ded into the living room, where my dad was reading the newspaper.

"Dad," I said, "Great-Grandpa Julius has something to say to you."

"Really?" said my dad. He put down his paper and turned toward the cat, with a big smile on his face. "All right," he said. "Tell me. What was the hardest part about changing from a person into a cat?"

Great-Grandpa Julius looked at my dad a moment without speaking. Then he **cock**ed his head, opened his mouth, and said, "For me, I guess the hardest part was finding out there wasn't a door you could **lock** behind you on the **litter** box. Is that good enough for a trip to Chicago?"

My dad's eyes looked like they were going to **pop** right out of his head.

"Sounds good enough to me," I said.

"How about you, Dad?"

Chapter 5

Once my dad found out my cat was Great-Grandpa Julius, he kept asking him questions about what it was like being dead. Dad never **let up** for the two days before we left for Chicago, and all during the long **ride** to the airport.

"Some people who died and were brought back to life again **claim** they went through what looked like a very long **tunnel** with very bright light at the other end," said my dad. "And all their dead **relative**s met them on the other side. Did that happen to you?"

"I do remember going through a long tunnel and coming out to bright light on the other side," said Great-Grandpa Julius from inside his cat carrying case.

"You do?" said my dad excitedly.

"Yes," said Great-Grandpa Julius. "It happened to be the Midtown Tunnel.[1] And the bright light on the other side was Queens.[2] That's where they **buried** me.

---

1 **Midtown Tunnel** 미드타운 터널. 뉴욕시의 이스트강(East River) 아래에 놓인 터널로, 맨해튼(Manhattan)과 퀸스(Queens), 두 자치구를 연결한다.

2 **Queens** 퀸스. 미국 뉴욕주(州) 뉴욕시에 속한 다섯 개의 자치구 가운데 하나.

Tell me something. Would you happen to have a cigar[3] on you? It's been years since I've smoked a really good cigar."

"You should stop smoking cigars," I said. "They're bad for you."

"I guess you're right," said Great-Grandpa Julius. "But some things you just don't stop **craving**, even after you're dead."

"How long have you been a cat?" asked my dad.

"I don't have a driver's **license** on me," said Great-Grandpa Julius. "How old do I look?"

"About twelve or thirteen," I said.

---

3 **cigar** 시가. 담뱃잎을 썰지 않고 통째로 돌돌 말아서 만든 담배.

"That feels about right," he said. "Of course, I didn't come back as a cat right away."

"You didn't?"

"Oh no. First I was a **caterpillar**."

"A caterpillar?" I said. "What was that like?"

"**Extreme**ly boring. Mostly it was about eating leaves. I ate leaves and tried to pretend they were herring with sour cream. Say,[4] you wouldn't **by any chance** happen to have a little schnapps[5] on you?"

"What's schnapps?" I asked.

"**Liquor**," said my dad. "No, I'm sorry, I

4　**say** 말을 처음 꺼낼 때 쓰는 표현으로 '저', '글쎄' 또는 '그러니까'라는 뜻이다.

5　**schnapps** 슈냅스. 곡식이나 감자 등으로 만든 독하고 색이 없으며 다양한 향을 내는 술.

don't carry schnapps on me."

We arrived at the airport. Dad paid the **cab** driver. I tried to put Great-Grandpa Julius back into his cat **carrier**.

"Hey, c'mon," he cried. "Don't make me travel in a **suitcase** again. I'm a **dignified** old **geezer**, for Pete's **sake**."

"In a past life you were a dignified old geezer," I said. "In *this* life you're a **stray** cat. And cats travel in cat carriers."

Julius **sigh**ed and got into his carrier.

Once we got on the plane, Dad started in again with his questions.

"So, Julius," said Dad, "after you were a caterpillar, did you become a butterfly?"

"No, a **moth**," said the voice inside the cat carrier. "Mostly that was about eating

sweaters."

"You ate sweaters?" I said. "Ugh!"

"Don't **knock** it till you've tried it," said
Great-Grandpa Julius. "I remember one
fine cashmere[6] turtleneck.[7] It was almost
as **tasty** as a corned beef[8] on **rye**. Then one
night I happened to fly a little too close to
a **torch** outside a Polynesian[9] restaurant
and—pffft!"

"Another tunnel?"

"No, no, moths don't get tunnels. Only
humans get tunnels. After that I became a

---

6 **cashmere** 캐시미어. 인도의 카슈미르(Kashmir) 지방에서 나는 산양의
털로 짠 고급 모직물. 부드럽고 윤기가 있으며, 보온성이 좋다.

7 **turtleneck** 긴 목 부분을 접어서 입는 스웨터.

8 **corned beef** 콘드 비프. 소고기를 소금이나 향신료 등에 절이고 쪄서 통
조림으로 만든 것.

9 **Polynesian** '폴리네시아의'라는 뜻. 폴리네시아는 태평양 중·남부에 펼
쳐 있는 여러 섬을 통틀어 이르는 말이다.

mouse."

"And that was all about eating cheese, I **suppose**," said my dad.

"No, about eating wood. Don't ask."

"Wait a minute," I said. "First you were a caterpillar, then you were a moth, then a mouse. How did you have time to be all those things?"

"We're not talking about a lot of time here," said Great-Grandpa Julius. "You could die, **do a stretch** as a caterpillar, then a moth, then a mouse, and you could still be back by a week from Thursday. But time didn't **matter** to me. I was dead. I had quite a lot of **leisure** time on my hands."

"Excuse me," said the **flight attendant**

as she passed our **row**. "In preparation for **takeoff**, please make sure your seat belts are **secure**ly **fasten**ed and that your seat backs and **tray** tables are in the **upright** and **lock**ed position."

"Hey, cookie,[10]" said Great-Grandpa Julius, "what are you doing after the flight?"

The flight attendant thought my dad said that, because she **gave** him **a dirty look**.

Then we **buckle**d up. Next stop— Chicago!

---

10 cookie 보통 귀여운 아이나 애인에게 애정을 담아 부르는 말.

"Before we see her, I just want to ask you one thing," said my dad in the elevator of the building on Lake **Shore** Drive where Grandma Leah lives.

"What's that?" I asked.

"Grandma Leah is in her eighties. Do you really think it's safe to tell a woman in her eighties that her dead father is now a cat?"

"Grandma Leah is a very **peppy, open-minded** person," I replied. "I'm sure she'll take the news OK."

The elevator doors opened on the seventh floor and we walked down the **hall** to Grandma Leah's apartment, my dad carrying our **luggage** and me carrying the carrier with Great-Grandpa Julius in it.

Grandma Leah was so happy to see us. She kept hugging and kissing us all over the place. When we were all **settle**d in her apartment she **notice**d the cat carrier for the first time.

"Don't tell me you brought an animal all the way to Chicago?" she said.

"Not just any animal, Grandma," I said. "A very special animal."

"Special in what way?" asked Grandma Leah.

"Special in the way that he is not only a cat, he is also a member of our family," I said.

"**In other words**, you love him so much you feel he's a member of our family?" asked Grandma Leah.

I looked at my dad and then back at Grandma Leah.

"No," I said, "I mean he really is a member of our family."

And with that I opened up the cat carrier. Grandma Leah and Great-Grandpa Julius took their first look at each other.

"Grandma Leah," I said, "I believe this is your father, Great-Grandpa Julius."

Grandma Leah **stare**d at the cat in silence for a moment and then shook her head.

"No," she said. "I don't believe it is. My father was taller."

"Leah **dear**," said Great-Grandpa Julius, "it's so wonderful to see you again. How have you been all these years, my **darling**?"

"It's talking to me," said Grandma Leah in a very strange voice. "A cat is talking to me in the English language."

"He is," I said.

"Leah dear," said Great-Grandpa Julius, "I may be a cat, but I'm also your father."

"It's still talking to me," said Grandma
Leah. "Am I right about this, that the cat is
still talking to me?"

"You're right," I said.

"Tell the cat I said it's not my father," she
said.

"Why don't you tell him yourself?" I
suggested.

"I don't talk to cats," said Grandma
Leah in the same strange voice.

"Grandma Leah says you're not her
father," I said.

"I *heard* her, I *heard* her," said Great-
Grandpa Julius. "What am I, **deaf**?" Then
the cat **soften**ed his voice. "Leah dear,
don't you remember me? It's Daddy!"

"Tell the cat I said that we never called

my father by the name of Daddy," said Grandma Leah. "Ask it what we called my real father."

"She says what name did she call you?" I asked.

"I heard her, I heard her." Great-Grandpa Julius's voice was rising. "You don't have to repeat everything she says."

"Well then, what name did she call you?"

"It wasn't Daddy," said Great-Grandpa Julius.

"We've already heard her say it wasn't Daddy," said my dad.

"Of course it wasn't Daddy," said Great-Grandpa Julius. "Because it was . . . Father."

Grandma Leah shook her head.

"Tell the cat it wasn't Father," said Grandma Leah.

"She says it wasn't—"

"Don't repeat it!" **snap**ped Great-Grandpa Julius angrily. Then he quickly **recover**ed his **composure**. "It wasn't Father. Of course it wasn't Father," he said. "Father was what I called myself. What you called me was . . . Papa."

"Tell the cat it wasn't Papa," said Grandma Leah.

"Oh boy," said Great-Grandpa Julius. "Could I ever use a good cigar or a glass of schnapps right about now. Leah dear, I'm over a hundred years old. I've been a **caterpillar**, a **moth**, a mouse. I've died many times, so my memory isn't quite what it used to be. Could you please **give** me **a break** here and tell me what you used to call me?"

"**Go on**, Grandma Leah," I said. "Tell him what you used to call him."

"I didn't call the *cat* anything," she said. "I called my *father*—my real father, my human father—Poppy."

"Poppy, shmoppy," said Great-Grandpa Julius. He **wave**d his **paw dismissive**ly. "How **far** is Poppy **from** Papa?"

"Wait a minute," said Grandma Leah. "I just **realize**d something."

"What's that?" I said.

"Did the cat say it wanted a good cigar or a glass of schnapps?"

"That's what he said," I said.

"My father, Julius, never smoked cigars. And he never drank schnapps. You know who smoked cigars and drank schnapps?"

"Who?" I said.

"Who?" said my dad.

"The **black sheep** of the family, that's who. Your cat is a liar, Zack. He's not my father, Julius, at all. He's your grandpa's **no-good** father. He's Great-Grandpa Maurice!"

"Is what Grandma Leah says true?" I **demand**ed of the large gray **tomcat**. "Are you my grandpa's **no-good** father, Maurice?"

"Now, **hold your horses**, sonny, hold your horses," he said. "First of all, where does she **get off** calling me a no-good?"

"Where do I get off?" said Grandma

Leah angrily. "I'll tell you where I get off. You took thirty thousand dollars of my father's money to **work on** your crazy **invent**ions. Then you left town. **Disappear**ed. We never heard a word from you again."

We all turned to the cat.

"What inventions?" I asked.

"I'll tell you what inventions," said Grandma Leah. "A **hairpiece** for **bald** eagles[1] was one."

"Who would ever buy a hairpiece for bald eagles?" I asked the cat.

"Well, that was a problem," said the cat.

---

1 **bald eagle** 흰머리수리. 북미 대륙에서 볼 수 있는 덩치가 매우 큰 맹금류로 미국을 상징하는 새이다. 머리에 난 흰 털 때문에 대머리처럼 보인다고 해서 대머리수리라고도 부른다.

"Then there was the dog **whistle**," Grandma Leah **went on**. "Only dogs **were supposed to** be able to hear it."

"That sounds better," I said.

"**Except** for one little thing," she said. The cat looked **embarrass**ed. "Dogs could not hear it either. You **blew** it and all the mice in the **neighbor**hood came running."

"Did you invent anything that worked?" I asked.

"Yes!" said the cat. "A sweater for dachshunds[2] in the shape of a hot dog[3] **bun**. Very cute, if I do say so myself. At first it didn't sell. I thought I'd lost

---

2 **dachshund** 닥스훈트. 허리가 길고 다리가 짧은 개.
3 **hot dog** 길쭉한 빵을 세로로 갈라 뜨거운 소시지 등을 안에 넣고 케첩이나 겨자 소스 등을 바른 음식.

all of Julius's money, so I **beat it** out of town. But you know what? After a while that sweater started selling like crazy. Everybody who owned a dachshund had to have one. I made back the whole thirty thousand. I had it sent directly to a secret bank **account** in Chicago."

"A secret bank account?" I said.

"In the Morton F. Acropolis Savings and **Loan Association**[4] of Chicago," said the cat. "I was coming to Chicago to pay Julius back when I got hit by a Greyhound bus.[5]"

We all **stare**d at the cat.

---

4 **savings and loan association** 우리나라의 상호 저축 은행에 해당하는 미국의 지역 금융 기관. 주로 주택 담보 대출을 운영한다.

5 **Greyhound bus** 그레이하운드 버스. 미국 전역과 캐나다 및 멕시코 일부 도시를 연결하는 많은 노선을 지닌 미국의 장거리 버스 회사 및 그 버스.

"Great-Grandpa Maurice," I said gently. "You've told us many things that weren't true. How do we know what you're telling us now is the truth?"

"First thing tomorrow morning," he said, "take me to the Morton F. Acropolis Savings and Loan Association of Chicago. Then you'll find out."

Chapter 8

And so the next morning, right after breakfast, my dad, my Grandma Leah, my Great-Grandpa Maurice, and I all got into a **cab** and went to the Morton F. Acropolis Savings and **Loan Association** of Chicago.

At first the bank **officer** we spoke with told us she couldn't find any secret bank **account bear**ing the number Maurice had given us.

"Tell her to look harder," said Maurice from inside the cat **carrier**.

The bank officer looked **startle**d.

"Please look harder, ma'am," I said.

And so the bank officer looked harder.

"You'd better be telling us the truth about this," I said to the cat carrier.

"Don't be so **mistrust**ful," said the voice from inside the cat carrier.

The bank officer returned.

"I did find something," she said. "An account was opened a great many years ago. I don't know if it's the right one. But it does bear the same number you gave me."

"What's the name on the account?" I asked.

"That, of course, would be a secret," said the bank officer.

"What if I told you the first name?" I said. "Would you just **nod** your head if I'm right?"

"What name are you thinking of?" she asked.

"Maurice," I said.

The bank officer nodded.

"I'm right!" I said. Great-Grandpa Maurice was telling the truth! "Now how do we get the money?"

"Well, the **individual** whose name is on the account would have to **sign** for it," she said.

We all looked at each other.

"What if he couldn't do that?" asked my

dad.

"Why couldn't he do that?" said the bank officer.

"What if he were . . . What if something had happened to him?" I said.

"Such as what?" said the bank officer.

"Such as, oh, I don't know, such as he turned into a cat," I said.

"Such as he *died*," said my dad quickly.

"Well, if the account holder is **decease**d," said the bank officer, "then the money would go into **probate**. Probate is a very long, very **complicate**d **legal process**. It takes years to **sort out**."

"What does deceased mean?" I **whisper**ed.

"Dead," said the voice inside the cat

carrier.

"What if he **turn**ed **into** a cat?" I asked.

"Excuse me?" said the bank officer.

My dad looked at me and shook his head.

"Do you believe in **reincarnation**?" I asked the bank officer.

"No," she said.

We all looked at each other. We didn't have any idea what to do next.

"Hey," said the voice in the cat carrier, "can I talk to her?"

"Is there somebody inside that animal carrier?" asked the bank officer, **alarm**ed.

"Hey, let me out of here!" said the voice.

I looked at my dad. He **shrug**ged. I

opened the cat carrier. Great-Grandpa Maurice **hop**ped out onto the **counter**.

"Uh, I'm afraid **pet**s aren't allowed inside the bank," said the bank officer, "The **regulation**s **specific**ally **forbid**—"

"Oh, **pipe down** a minute, sis,[1]" said Great-Grandpa Maurice. "And maybe we can **clear** this **up**."

The bank officer looked like she might **faint**.

"This," I said, "is my great-grandfather, Maurice. He opened the account with your bank many years ago when he was still a person."

The bank officer **lean**ed heavily against

---

1 **sis** 젊은 여자를 부르는 비격식적인 호칭.

the counter so she wouldn't fall down.

"This individual does, indeed, appear to be . . . a cat," she whispered.

"You're darned tootin'[2] I am," said Great-Grandpa Maurice. "And if you don't mind, I'd like to **withdraw** all the money in my account and give it to my family."

"Are you able to . . . sign for it?" she whispered, **barely** able to speak.

"Hey, dollface,[3]" he said, "I'm a cat. Maybe you **notice**d. I don't happen to have an **opposable thumb**.[4] So I can't hold a pen."

---

2 **darned tootin'** 다른 사람의 말에 동의할 때 사용하는 속어.

3 **dollface** 보통 젊은 여자나 어린아이를 부를 때 쓰는 호칭.

4 **opposable thumb** 인간이나 침팬지 등 영장류의 특징으로 다른 네 손가락과 마주 보는 엄지손가락을 의미한다. 단순히 물건을 잡는 일도 이런 엄지손가락이 있어서 가능하다.

"If you're unable to sign," she whispered, "we would be unable to . . . give you the money."

"Why the heck[5] not?" he asked.

"It would not be . . . **consistent** with company **policy**," she whispered, her eyes now **squeeze**d shut.

"Then how's about changing company policy?" he said. "From now on, anytime somebody gets reincarnated as a cat and comes in to get his money, all he has to do is ask for it. What do you say?"

The bank officer took a deep breath.

"I just don't . . . know if we can do that," she said.

---

5 **heck** '도대체', '젠장' 또는 '제기랄'이라는 뜻으로 당혹스럽거나 짜증스러운 감정을 강조하는 속어.

"OK then, get me Morty," said Great-Grandpa Maurice.

"Who's Morty?" asked the bank officer.

"Who's Morty?" repeated Great-Grandpa Maurice. "You mean to say you don't know Morton F. Acropolis, the **found**er of the bank?"

And with that, the cat **leap**t off the counter and **hotfoot**ed **it** down the **hall**.

"Now just a minute there," the bank officer called after him. "I can't let you—"

Great-Grandpa Maurice stopped in front of a **fancy** door. It said "Morton F. Acropolis" on the front.

"Hey, Morty!" **yell**ed Great-Grandpa Maurice. "You in there?"

"Maurice?" called a surprised voice

from inside the office. "Maurice, is that you?"

The cat pushed the founder's door open with his nose and walked inside. My dad, Grandma Leah, and I followed close behind. The bank officer came right after us.

Behind a long desk that looked like some kind of **antique** sat the oldest man I had ever seen. He was also one of the shortest. I **doubt** if he was a lot taller than me, and he had on a pair of glasses with **amazing**ly thick lenses.

"Hey, Morty, great to see you!" said the cat.

"Maurice, you old dog,[6] is that you?" cried Mr. Acropolis. He **squint**ed through

Merton F. Acropolis
Founder

his glasses and **peer**ed over the top of his desk. "My eyes aren't what they used to be. But I'd **recognize** that voice anywhere, even after all these years!"

"So how have you been, Morty?"

"**Never mind** me, what about you, Maurice? I heard you were dead."

"I was," said the cat. "But I'm better now. Listen, Morty, I got a problem. Maybe you can help me."

"For you, Maurice? Anything. What can I do?"

"Sir," said the bank officer, "do you **realize** you're talking to a c—"

"Quiet, Lola," **snap**ped the old man. "I

---

6 **dog** 남자를 가리키는 속어로 '녀석', '놈'이라는 뜻.

haven't seen this man in ages."

"But he's not a man, sir," said the bank officer, "he's a c—"

"Quiet!" shouted Mr. Acropolis. "Go ahead, Maurice, what can I do for you?"

"It's the money I made on the hot dog sweater, Morty. I'd like to withdraw it from my account. But this young lady here tells me I can't."

"**Poppycock**!" **roar**ed Mr. Acropolis. "I **invest**ed in that hot dog sweater myself. Smartest move I ever made. Give the man his money, Lola!"

"But, Mr. Acropolis, he's unable to sign for it."

"Why's that?"

"He can't hold a pen in his **paw**s," she

said.

"Well, I can't hold a pen in *my* paws either," said Mr. Acropolis. "A man gets to be our age, **dear**, there are certain things he can't do by himself any longer. Help him, for the love of Pete![7]"

"Y-yes, sir," said the bank officer.

And so we all walked out of Mr. Acropolis's office. Then, with shaking hands, the bank officer put a pen between the cat's paws and helped him sign his name. Then she wrote out a check and handed it to us. My dad looked at the amount and **whistle**d.

"Maurice, I thought you said there was

---

7 **for the love of Pete** '제발', '부디'라는 뜻으로 간청하거나 애원할 때 쓰는 표현.

thirty thousand dollars in this account," he said.

"How much is in there?" asked Maurice.

"Closer to ninety," said my dad.

"Ninety thousand dollars?" asked Grandma Leah. It was the first thing she'd said since we'd arrived at the bank.

"Well, that's after more than thirty years of **interest**," said my dad.

"And you really want us to have this?" I asked.

"On one **condition**," said Maurice.

"What's that?"

"That you leave me enough for a first-class, one-way ticket to Palm Beach,[8] and a few years' **rent** in a **deluxe** pet hotel, with a

standing order for herring and sour cream every morning, and a glass of schnapps every night."

"You're not going to live with us?" I said.

"As much as I love you, Zack," said Maurice, "I've always wanted to spend my **golden years** in Florida. I understand there are **folk**s down there who might be **willing** to invest a few dollars in **invent**ions of a somewhat **speculative nature**."

So Maurice went off to live the good life in Florida. But before he did he had the bank

8 **Palm Beach** 팜비치. 미국 플로리다주(州)의 남동부에 있는 도시. 겨울철 휴양을 위해 많이 찾는 곳이다.

officer open his safe-**deposit** box.[9] There it was. A baseball signed by Lou Gehrig, Ty Cobb, and Rogers Hornsby.

"This is for you, kid," he said to me. "I was going to keep it, but hey, what the heck does an old **pussycat** need with an old baseball anyway?"

Even though Great-Grandpa Maurice was kind of **pushy**, I was really sad to see him go.

"Hey, Zack," he said, "**cheer up**. Now you can go back to the animal **shelter** and get that little tuxedo **kitten** you were looking at."

"But you said he has **flea**s and **worm**s

---

9 **safe-deposit box** 은행에서 귀중품 보관을 위해 개인에게 대여해 주는 안전 금고.

and never learned how to use a **litter** box," I replied.

"Maybe so," he said. "But there's one thing about him that might make you **overlook** all that."

"What?"

"In a **former** life he was Babe Ruth.[10]"

---

10 **Babe Ruth** 베이브 루스. 본명은 조지 허먼 루스(George Herman Ruth)로 미국에서 가장 인기가 많았던 프로 야구 선수이자 메이저리그를 대표하는 홈런 타자이다.

THE ZACK FILES
Great-Grandpa's in the
Litter Box

THE ZACK FILES™

Great-Grandpa's in the Litter Box

CONTENTS

평범한 소년이 겪는 기상천외하고 흥미로운 모험을 그린 이야기, 잭 파일스!

『잭 파일스(The Zack Files)』 시리즈는 뉴욕에 사는 평범한 소년 잭이 겪는 때로는 으스스하고, 때로는 우스꽝스러운 모험을 담고 있습니다. 저자 댄 그린버그(Dan Greenburg)는 자신의 아들 잭에게서 영감을 받아 그를 주인공으로 한 이야기를 떠올렸고, 잭과 같은 아이들이 독서에 흥미를 갖기를 바라는 마음을 담아 이 책을 썼습니다.

초자연적인 현상에 대한 저자의 관심을 녹여 낸『잭 파일스』 시리즈는 누구나 한 번쯤은 들어 본 기괴한 이야기들을 아이들이 재미있게 읽을 수 있도록 흥미진진하게 소개하고 있습니다. 현재까지 총 30권의 책이 출간되어 전 세계 아이들의 호기심을 불러일으키고 있으며, 동명의 TV 드라마로도 제작되어 많은 관심과 사랑을 받기도 했습니다.

이러한 이유로『잭 파일스』 시리즈는 '엄마표 · 아빠표 영어'를 진행하는 부모님과 초보 영어 학습자라면 반드시 읽어야 하는 영어원서로 자리 잡았습니다. 간결한 어휘로 재치 있게 풀어 쓴 이야기는 영어원서가 친숙하지 않은 학습자들에게도 즐거운 원서 읽기 경험을 선사할 것입니다.

번역과 단어장이 포함된 워크북, 그리고 오디오북까지 담긴 풀 패키지!

이 책은 영어원서『잭 파일스』 시리즈에, 탁월한 학습 효과를 거둘 수 있도록 다양한 콘텐츠를 덧붙인 책입니다.

- **영어원서**: 본문에 나온 어려운 어휘에 볼드 처리가 되어 있어 단어를 더욱 분명하게 인지할 수 있고, 문맥에 따른 자연스러운 암기 효과를 얻을 수 있습니다.
- **단어장**: 원서에 볼드 처리된 어휘의 의미가 완벽하게 정리되어 있어 사전 없이 원서를 수월하게 읽을 수 있으며, 반복해서 등장하는 단어에 '복습' 표기를 하여 자연스럽게 복습을 돕도록 구성했습니다.
- **번역**: 영문과 비교할 수 있도록 직역에 가까운 번역을 담았습니다. 원서 읽기에 익숙하지 않은 초보 학습자도 어려움 없이 내용을 파악할 수 있습니다.
- **퀴즈**: 챕터별로 내용을 확인하는 이해력 점검 퀴즈가 들어 있습니다.
- **오디오북**: 본문 전체에 대한 오디오북을 포함하고 있어, 듣기 훈련은 물론

소리 내어 읽기에까지 폭넓게 사용할 수 있습니다.

『잭 파일스』 이렇게 읽어 보세요!

- **단어 암기는 이렇게!** 처음 리딩을 시작하기 전, 오늘 읽을 챕터에 나오는 단어들을 눈으로 쭉 훑어봅니다. 모르는 단어는 좀 더 주의 깊게 보되, 손으로 쓰면서 완벽하게 암기할 필요는 없습니다. 본문을 읽으면서 이 단어를 다시 만나게 되는데, 그 과정에서 단어의 쓰임새와 어감을 자연스럽게 익히게 됩니다. 이렇게 책을 읽은 후에 단어를 다시 한번 복습하세요. 복습할 때는 중요하다고 생각하는 단어들을 손으로 쓰면서 꼼꼼하게 외우는 것도 좋습니다. 이런 방식으로 책을 읽으면 많은 단어를 빠르고 부담 없이 익힐 수 있습니다.

- **리딩할 때는 리딩에만 집중하자!** 원서를 읽는 중간중간 모르는 단어가 나온다고 워크북을 바로 펼쳐 보거나, 곧바로 번역을 찾아보는 것은 크게 도움이 되지 않습니다. 모르는 단어나 이해되지 않는 문장들은 따로 가볍게 표시만 해 두고, 전체적인 맥락을 파악하며 속도감 있게 읽어 나가세요. 리딩을 할 때는 속도에 대한 긴장감을 잃지 않으면서 리딩에만 집중하는 것이 좋습니다. 모르는 단어와 문장은 리딩을 마친 후에 한꺼번에 정리하는 '리뷰' 시간을 통해 점검하는 시간을 가지면 됩니다. 리뷰를 할 때는 번역은 물론 단어장과 사전도 꼼꼼하게 확인하면서 어떤 이유에서 이해가 되지 않았는지 생각해 봅니다.

- **번역 활용은 이렇게!** 이해가 가지 않는 문장은 번역을 통해서 그 의미를 파악할 수 있습니다. 하지만 한국어와 영어는 정확히 1:1 대응이 되지 않기 때문에 번역을 활용하는 데에도 지혜가 필요합니다. 의역이 된 부분까지 억지로 의미를 대응해서 이해하려고 하기보다, 어떻게 그런 의미가 만들어진 것인지 추측하면서 번역은 참고 자료로 활용하는 것이 좋습니다.

- **듣기 훈련은 이렇게!** 리스닝 실력을 향상시키고 싶다면 오디오북을 적극적으로 활용해 보세요. 처음에는 오디오북을 틀어 놓고 눈으로 해당 내용을 따라 읽으면서 훈련을 하고, 이것이 익숙해지면 오디오북만 틀어 놓고 '귀를 통해' 책을 읽어 보세요. 눈으로 읽지 않은 책이라도 귀를 통해 이해할 수 있을 정도가

되면, 이후에 영어 듣기로 어려움을 겪는 일은 거의 없을 것입니다.

- **2~3번 반복해서 읽자!** 영어 초보자라면 처음부터 완벽하게 이해하려고 하는 것보다는 2~3회 반복해서 읽을 것을 추천합니다. 처음 원서를 읽을 때는 생소한 단어들과 스토리 때문에 내용 파악에 급급할 수밖에 없습니다. 하지만 일단 내용을 파악한 후에 다시 읽으면 문장 구조나 어휘의 활용에 더 집중하게 되고, 원서를 더 깊이 있게 읽을 수 있습니다. 그 과정에서 리딩 속도에 탄력이 붙고 리딩 실력 또한 더 확고히 다지게 됩니다.

- **'시리즈'로 꾸준히 읽자!** 한 작가의 책을 시리즈로 읽는 것 또한 영어 실력 향상에 큰 도움이 됩니다. 같은 등장인물이 다시 나오기 때문에 내용 파악이 더 수월할 뿐 아니라, 작가가 사용하는 어휘와 표현들도 반복되기 때문에 탁월한 복습 효과까지 얻을 수 있습니다. 롱테일북스의 『잭 파일스』 시리즈는 현재 6권, 총 31,441단어 분량이 출간되어 있습니다. 시리즈를 꾸준히 읽다 보면 영어 실력이 자연스럽게 향상될 것입니다.

원서 본문 구성

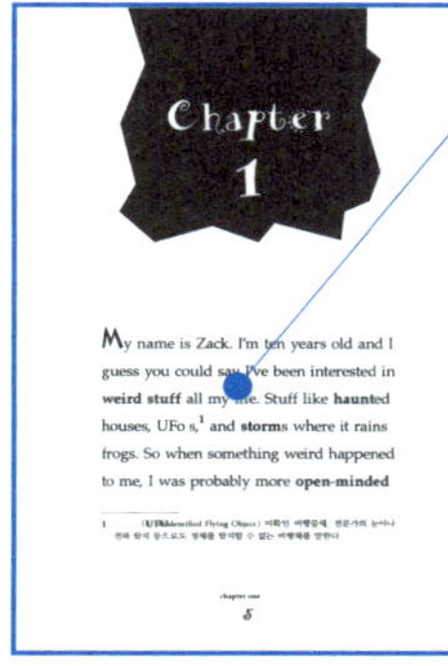

내용이 담긴 원서 본문입니다.

원어민이 읽는 일반 원서와 같은 텍스트지만, 암기해야 할 중요 어휘들은 볼드체로 표시되어 있습니다. 이 어휘들은 지금 들고 계신 워크북에 챕터별로 정리되어 있습니다.

학습 심리학 연구 결과에 따르면, 한 단어씩 따로 외우는 단어 암기는 거의 효과가 없다고 합니다. 단어를 제대로 외우기 위해서는 문맥(context) 속에서 단어를 암기해야 하며, 한 단어당 문맥 속에서 15번 이상 마주칠 때 완벽하게 암기할 수 있다고 합니다.

이 책의 본문에서는 중요 어휘를 볼드체로 강조하여, 문맥 속의 단어들을 더 확실히 인지(word cognition in context)하도록 돕고 있습니다. 또한 대부분의 중요 단어들은 다른 챕터에서도 반복해서 등장하기 때문에 이 책을 읽는 것만으로도 자연스럽게 어휘력을 향상시킬 수 있습니다.

본문 하단에는 내용 이해를 돕기 위한 '각주'가 첨가되어 있습니다. 각주는 굳이 암기할 필요는 없지만, 알아 두면 도움이 될 만한 정보를 설명하고 있습니다. 각주를 참고하면 스토리를 더 깊이 있게 이해할 수 있어 원서를 읽는 재미가 배가됩니다.

워크북(Workbook) 구성

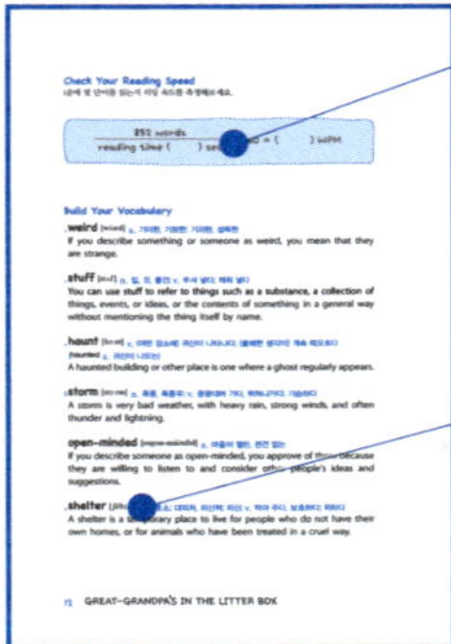

Check Your Reading Speed

해당 챕터의 단어 수가 기록되어 있어, 리딩 속도를 측정할 수 있습니다. 특히 리딩 속도를 중시하는 독자들이 유용하게 사용할 수 있습니다.

Build Your Vocabulary

본문에 볼드 표시되어 있는 단어들이 정리되어 있습니다. 리딩 전 · 후에 반복해서 보면 원서를 더욱 쉽게 읽을 수 있고, 어휘력도 빠르게 향상될 것입니다.

단어는 〈스펠링 – 빈도 – 발음기호 – 품사 – 한글 뜻 – 영문 뜻〉 순서로 표기되어 있으며 빈도 표시(★)가 많을수록 필수 어휘입니다. 반복해서 등장하는 단어는 빈도 대신 '복습'으로 표기되어 있습니다. 품사는 아래와 같이 표기했습니다.

n. 명사 │ **a.** 형용사 │ **ad.** 부사 │ **v.** 동사

conj. 접속사 │ **prep.** 전치사 │ **int.** 감탄사 │ **idiom** 숙어 및 관용구

Comprehension Quiz

간단한 퀴즈를 통해 읽은 내용에 대한 이해력을 점검해 볼 수 있습니다.

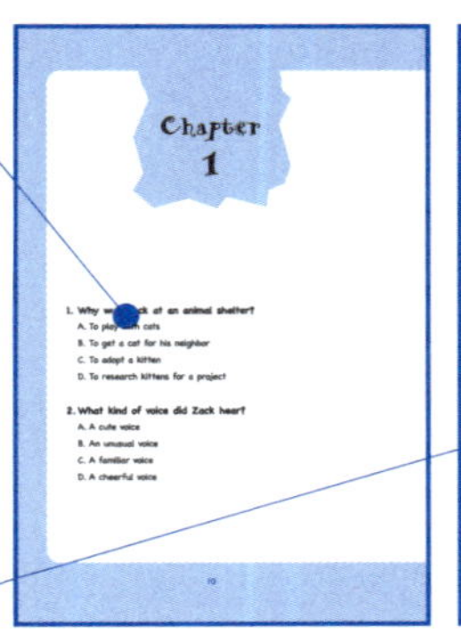

한국어 번역

영문과 비교할 수 있도록 최대한 직역에 가까운 번역을 담았습니다.

이 책의 수준과 타깃 독자

- 미국 원어민 기준: 유치원 ~ 초등학교 저학년
- 한국 학습자 기준: 초등학교 저학년 ~ 중학생
- 영어원서 완독 경험이 없는 초보 영어 학습자
- 도서 분량: 약 5,000단어
- 비슷한 수준의 다른 챕터북: Arthur Chapter Book★, Flat Stanley★, Tales from the Odyssey★, Junie B. Jones★, Magic Tree House, Marvin Redpost

  ★「롱테일 에디션」으로 이미 출간된 도서

QR 코드를 인식하여 「잭 파일스」 1권 원서 오디오북을 들어 보세요! 더불어 롱테일북스 홈페이지(www.longtailbooks.co.kr)에서도 오디오북 MP3 파일을 다운로드 받을 수 있습니다.

1. Why was Zack at an animal shelter?

    A. To play with cats

    B. To get a cat for his neighbor

    C. To adopt a kitten

    D. To research kittens for a project

2. What kind of voice did Zack hear?

    A. A cute voice

    B. An unusual voice

    C. A familiar voice

    D. A cheerful voice

3. **What did Zack first think of the talking cat?**

A. He thought the cat was strangely polite.

B. He felt like the cat was very dangerous.

C. He assumed the cat was part of a dream.

D. He was not sure the cat was really talking.

4. **What was true about the tomcat?**

A. He was not about to die.

B. He had never used a litter box.

C. He was friends with the tuxedo kitten.

D. He was born in the animal shelter.

5. **How did the tomcat know Zack's name?**

A. He had heard someone say it.

B. He was one of Zack's relatives.

C. He could read human minds.

D. He had read about Zack in the newspaper.

1분에 몇 단어를 읽는지 리딩 속도를 측정해보세요.

$$\frac{852 \text{ words}}{\text{reading time (} \quad \text{) sec}} \times 60 = (\quad) \text{ WPM}$$

Build Your Vocabulary

★ **weird** [wiərd] a. 기이한, 기묘한; 기괴한, 섬뜩한
If you describe something or someone as weird, you mean that they are strange.

★ **stuff** [stʌf] n. 일, 것, 물건; v. 쑤셔 넣다; 채워 넣다
You can use stuff to refer to things such as a substance, a collection of things, events, or ideas, or the contents of something in a general way without mentioning the thing itself by name.

★ **haunt** [hɔ:nt] v. (어떤 장소에) 귀신이 나타나다; (불쾌한 생각이) 계속 떠오르다
(haunted a. 귀신이 나오는)
A haunted building or other place is one where a ghost regularly appears.

⁑ **storm** [stɔ:rm] n. 폭풍, 폭풍우; v. 쿵쾅대며 가다, 뛰쳐나가다; 기습하다
A storm is very bad weather, with heavy rain, strong winds, and often thunder and lightning.

open-minded [oupən-máindid] a. 마음이 열린, 편견 없는
If you describe someone as open-minded, you approve of them because they are willing to listen to and consider other people's ideas and suggestions.

★ **shelter** [ʃéltər] n. 보호소; 대피처, 피신처; 피신; v. 막아 주다, 보호하다; 피하다
A shelter is a temporary place to live for people who do not have their own homes, or for animals who have been treated in a cruel way.

beg [beg] v. 간청하다, 애원하다; 구걸하다
If you beg someone to do something, you ask them very anxiously or
eagerly to do it.

break down idiom 굴복하다; 무너지다; 고장 나다; 실패하다
If you break down, you agree to do what someone wants or to accept
what they do.

kitten [kitn] n. [동물] 새끼 고양이
A kitten is a very young cat.

cage [keidʒ] n. 우리; 새장; v. 우리에 가두다
A cage is a structure of wire or metal bars in which birds or animals are
kept.

tomcat [támkæt] n. [동물] 수고양이
A tomcat is a male cat.

fur [fə:r] n. (동물의) 털; 모피
Fur is the thick and usually soft hair that grows on the bodies of many
mammals.

matted [mǽtid] a. 엉겨붙은, 들러붙은
If you describe someone's hair as matted, you mean that it has become
a thick untidy mass, often because it is wet or dirty.

dirt [də:rt] n. 먼지, 때; 흙
If there is dirt on something, there is dust, mud, or a stain on it.

whisker [wískər] n. (고양이·쥐 등의) 수염; (pl.) 구레나룻
The whiskers of an animal such as a cat or a mouse are the long stiff
hairs that grow near its mouth.

lopsided [lápsaidid] a. 한쪽이 처진
Something that is lopsided is uneven because one side is lower or
heavier than the other.

tip [tip] n. (뾰족한) 끝; 조언; v. 기울어지다; 살짝 건드리다
The tip of something long and narrow is the end of it.

* **chew** [ʧuː] v. 물어뜯다, 깨물다; (음식을) 씹다; n. 씹기, 깨물기
If a person or animal chews an object, they bite it with their teeth.

raspy [rǽspi] a. (목소리가) 거친, 목이 쉰 듯한
If someone has a raspy voice, they make rough sounds as if they have a
sore throat or have difficulty in breathing.

‡ **sight** [sait] n. 시야; 광경, 모습; 보기; v. 갑자기 보다
If something is in sight or within sight, you can see it.

* **paw** [pɔː] n. (동물의) 발; (사람의) 손; v. 발로 긁다; (함부로) 건드리다
The paws of an animal such as a cat, dog, or bear are its feet, which have
claws for gripping things and soft pads for walking on.

* **nap** [næp] n. 잠깐 잠, 낮잠; v. 잠깐 자다, 낮잠을 자다
If you have a nap, you have a short sleep, usually during the day.

‡ **adopt** [ədápt] v. 입양하다; (태도·어조·표정 등을) 취하다
If you adopt an animal, you take an animal that has been left in a place
such as a rescue center, and keep it as your pet.

‡ **neighbor** [néibər] n. 이웃 (사람); v. 이웃하다, 인접하다
Your neighbor is someone who lives near you.

take a chance idiom 위험을 무릅쓰다, 운에 맡기다
When you take a chance, you try to do something although there is a
large risk of danger or failure.

dummy [dʌ́mi] n. 멍청이, 바보; 인체 모형; a. 모조의, 가짜의
If you call someone a dummy, you are indicating that they are stupid
or silly.

scruffy [skrʌ́fi] a. 꾀죄죄한, 지저분한
Someone or something that is scruffy is dirty and untidy.

* **stare** [stɛər] v. 빤히 쳐다보다, 응시하다; n. 빤히 쳐다보기, 응시
If you stare at someone or something, you look at them for a long time.

cross [krɔːs] a. 짜증난, 약간 화가 난; v. (가로질러) 건너다; n. 십자 기호
(crossly ad. 심술궂게)
Someone who is cross is rather angry or irritated.

pardon [paːrdn] v. 용서하다, 눈감아주다; n. 용서
If you pardon someone for something, you forgive them for something
they have said or done.

holler [hálər] v. 소리지르다, 고함치다; n. 고함, 외침
If you holler, you shout loudly.

be about to idiom 막 ~하려는 참이다
If you are about to do something, you are going to do it immediately.

hardly [háːrdli] ad. 거의 ~할 수가 없다; ~하자마자; 거의 ~아니다
When you say you can hardly do something, you are emphasizing that
it is very difficult for you to do it.

believe one's ears idiom 들은 것을 그대로 정말이라고 믿다
If you cannot believe your ears, you are so surprised by what you hear
that you think you are imagining it.

lip [lip] n. 입술
Your lips are the two outer parts of the edge of your mouth.

trick [trik] n. 속임수; 솜씨, 재주; 요령; v. 속이다, 속임수를 쓰다
A trick is an action that is intended to deceive someone.

far out [faːr áut] a. 기발한, 이색적인; 과격한, 극단적인
If you describe something as far out, you mean that it is very strange
or extreme.

sarcastic [saːrkǽstik] a. 빈정대는, 비꼬는; 풍자적인 (sarcastically ad. 비꼬는 투로)
Someone who is sarcastic says or does the opposite of what they really
mean in order to mock or insult someone.

stand [stænd] v. 참다, 견디다; 서다
If you cannot stand someone or something, you dislike them very
strongly.

meow [miáu] v. (고양이가) 야옹 하고 울다; n. 야옹 (하고 우는 소리)
If a cat meows, it makes a crying sound.

drive up the wall idiom ~을 몹시 짜증나게 하다
If you say that something or someone is driving you up the wall, you are
emphasizing that they annoy and irritate you.

bossy [bɔ́:si] a. 이래라저래라 하는, 대장 행세하는
If you describe someone as bossy, you mean that they enjoy telling
people what to do.

⋆ **flea** [fli:] n. 벼룩
A flea is a very small jumping insect that has no wings and feeds on the
blood of humans or animals.

⁑ **worm** [wə:rm] n. 기생충; (땅 속에 사는) 벌레; v. 꿈틀거리며 나아가다
If animals or people have worms, worms are living in their intestines.

get the hang of idiom ~을 할 줄 알게 되다; 요령을 알다
If you get the hang of something such as a skill or activity, you begin to
understand or realize how to do it.

⋆ **litter** [lítər] n. (애완동물의 대소변용) 깔개; 쓰레기; v. 흐트러져 어지럽히다
(litter box n. 애완동물용 변기)
Litter is a dry substance that you put in the container where you want
your cat to go to the toilet.

⁑ **buy** [bai] v. (발언·변명 등을) 믿다, 그대로 받아들이다; 사다
If you buy an idea or a theory, you believe and accept it.

go on idiom 말을 계속하다; (어떤 상황이) 계속되다; 자자, 어서
If you go on, you continue saying something or talking about something.

put to sleep idiom (병들거나 다친 동물을) 안락사시키다
If you put a sick or injured animal to sleep, you give it drugs so that it
dies quickly without feeling any pain.

tuck [tʌk] v. (따뜻하게) 덮어 주다; 집어넣다; 밀어 넣다; n. 주름, 단

If you tuck someone, especially a child, in bed, you make them comfortable in bed by arranging the covers around them.

jammies [dʒǽmiz] n. (= pajamas) 잠옷

Jammies refer to a pair of pajamas which consists of loose trousers and a loose jacket that people wear in bed in a childish way.

conscience [kánʃəns] n. 양심; (양심의) 가책

Your conscience is the part of your mind that tells you whether what you are doing is right or wrong.

well-known [wel-nóun] a. 유명한, 잘 알려진; 친한, 친숙한

A well-known fact is a fact that is known by people in general.

admit [ædmít] v. 인정하다, 시인하다; 받아들이다

If you admit that something bad, unpleasant, or embarrassing is true, you agree, often unwillingly, that it is true.

impress [imprés] v. 깊은 인상을 주다, 감동을 주다 (impressed a. 감명을 받은)

If something impresses you, you feel great admiration for it.

reincarnate [rìːinkáːrneit] v. 환생시키다 (reincarnation n. 환생)

If you believe in reincarnation, you believe that you will be born again and will live in the body of another person or animal after you die.

claim [kleim] v. (~이 사실이라고) 주장하다; 요구하다; n. 청구; 주장

If you say that someone claims that something is true, you mean they say that it is true but you are not sure whether or not they are telling the truth.

ordinary [ɔ́ːrdənèri] a. 보통의, 평범한

Ordinary people or things are normal and not special or different in any way.

Chapter 2

1. **How did Zack first feel about the situation?**

   A. He was delighted that he could talk to a cat.

   B. He was certain that he should adopt the kitten.

   C. He felt lucky to have found his great-grandfather.

   D. He felt hesitant to take the tomcat home.

2. **What did the tomcat think of the kitten?**

   A. The kitten was not that impressive.

   B. The kitten was incredibly precious.

   C. The kitten was so selfish.

   D. The kitten was obviously lonely.

3. **From Zack's perspective, how did the tomcat and kitten compare?**

   A. The kitten was not as innocent as the tomcat.

   B. The kitten was more unpredictable than the tomcat.

   C. The tomcat was not as attractive as the kitten.

   D. The tomcat was more charming than the kitten.

4. **What was the tomcat's opinion on family?**

   A. Family was more important than strangers.

   B. Family should always help strangers.

   C. Supporting one's family was optional.

   D. Being with one's family was annoying.

5. **What made Zack decide to take the tomcat?**

   A. He lost interest in the kitten.

   B. He thought of his grandmother.

   C. He felt sorry for the tomcat.

   D. He wanted to make his parents proud.

1분에 몇 단어를 읽는지 리딩 속도를 측정해보세요.

$$\frac{186 \text{ words}}{\text{reading time (\quad) sec}} \times 60 = (\qquad) \text{ WPM}$$

Build Your Vocabulary

복습 **be about to** idiom 막 ~하려는 참이다
If you are about to do something, you are going to do it immediately.

복습 **kitten** [kitn] n. [동물] 새끼 고양이
A kitten is a very young cat.

복습 **tomcat** [támkæt] n. [동물] 수고양이
A tomcat is a male cat.

★ **lick** [lik] v. 핥다; 핥아먹다; n. 한 번 핥기, 핥아먹기
When people or animals lick something, they move their tongue across its surface.

복습 **paw** [pɔː] n. (동물의) 발; (사람의) 손; v. 발로 긁다; (함부로) 건드리다
The paws of an animal such as a cat, dog, or bear are its feet, which have claws for gripping things and soft pads for walking on.

adorable [ədɔ́ːrəbl] a. 사랑스러운
If you say that someone or something is adorable, you are emphasizing that they are very attractive and you feel great affection for them.

lean toward idiom ~쪽으로 (마음이) 기울어지다
If you lean toward something, you are interested in it and are likely to do a particular activity.

* **pose** [pouz] v. 포즈를 취하다; (위협·문제 등을) 제기하다; n. 포즈, 자세
If you pose for a photograph or painting, you stay in a particular position so that someone can photograph you or paint you.

복습 **flea** [fliː] n. 벼룩
A flea is a very small jumping insect that has no wings and feeds on the blood of humans or animals.

* **bite** [bait] v. (bit-bitten) (곤충 등이) 물다; (이빨로) 물다; n. 한 입; 물기; 소량
If a snake or a small insect bites you, it makes a mark or hole in your skin, and often causes the surrounding area of your skin to become painful or itchy.

* **proper** [prápər] a. 적절한, 제대로 된; 올바른 (properly ad. 제대로, 적절히)
If something is done properly, it is done in a correct and satisfactory way.

toilet-train [tɔ́ilit-trèin] v. 용변을 가리는 연습을 시키다
(toilet-trained a. 용변을 가릴 줄 아는)
If a child is toilet trained, he or she has learned to use the toilet.

* **beloved** [bilʌ́vid] a. (대단히) 사랑하는; 총애 받는; 인기 많은
A beloved person, thing, or place is one that you feel great affection for.

* **rot** [rat] v. 썩다; 썩히다, 부식시키다; n. 썩음, 부식, 부패
If you say that someone is being left to rot in a particular place, especially in a prison, you mean that they are being left there and their physical and mental condition is being allowed to get worse and worse.

stink [stiŋk] v. (고약한) 냄새가 나다; 수상쩍다; n. 악취 (stinking a. 악취가 나는)
To stink means to smell extremely unpleasant.

복습 **cage** [keidʒ] n. 우리; 새장; v. 우리에 가두다
A cage is a structure of wire or metal bars in which birds or animals are kept.

talk sense idiom 이치에 맞는 말을 하다
If you say that someone talks sense, you mean that what they say is sensible.

Chapter 3

1. **How did Zack's dad react when Zack said that the cat could talk?**

   A. He figured Zack was kidding.

   B. He immediately believed Zack.

   C. He got mad at Zack for lying.

   D. He was completely shocked.

2. **What did Grandma Leah used to say about her family?**

   A. Her father, Julius, was a sweet person.

   B. Her father, Julius, caused a lot of trouble.

   C. Her husband's father, Maurice, hated her.

   D. Her husband's father, Maurice, was her role model.

3. **What did Zack's dad do when he saw the cat?**

    A. He told the cat that he looked old.

    B. He pretended the cat was Great-Grandpa Julius.

    C. He demanded the cat prove his identity.

    D. He asked the cat who his favorite relative was.

4. **Why didn't Great-Grandpa Julius talk to Zack's dad?**

    A. He did not know what to say.

    B. He was worried he would sound foolish.

    C. He was capable of speaking only to Zack.

    D. He talked only when he felt like it.

5. **Why was Great-Grandpa Julius unhappy?**

    A. He wanted to go back to the animal shelter.

    B. He wanted a more comfortable place to sleep.

    C. He wanted food that Zack did not have.

    D. He just wanted to be alone.

1분에 몇 단어를 읽는지 리딩 속도를 측정해보세요.

$$\frac{540 \text{ words}}{\text{reading time (} \quad \text{) sec}} \times 60 = (\quad) \text{ WPM}$$

Build Your Vocabulary

huff and puff idiom (몹시 지쳐서) 헉헉거리다; (짜증이 나서) 씩씩대다
If you huff and puff, you breathe heavily while making a great physical effort.

⋆**carrier** [kǽriər] n. 나르는 것; 항공사, 수송회사; 보균자
Pet carriers are small portable boxes, crates, or cages used to transport small animals such as cats or lap dogs from one location to another.

⋆**split** [split] v. (split–split) 헤어지다; 분열되다; 나뉘다; n. 분열; 분할
(split up idiom 헤어지다)
If two people split up, they end their relationship or marriage.

kitty [kíti] n. [동물] 고양이
Kitty is used to call a kitten or cat in an informal way.

⋆**exhaust** [igzɔ́:st] v. 기진맥진하게 하다; 다 써 버리다; n. (자동차 등의) 배기가스
(exhausted a. 기진맥진한)
If something exhausts you, it makes you so tired, either physically or mentally, that you have no energy left.

⋆**weigh** [wei] v. 무게가 ~이다; 무게를 달다
If someone or something weighs a particular amount, this amount is how heavy they are.

⋆**slight** [slait] a. 약간의, 조금의; 작고 여윈 (slightly ad. 약간, 조금)
Slightly means to some degree but not to a very large degree.

ordinary [ɔ́:rdənèri] a. 보통의, 평범한
Ordinary people or things are normal and not special or different in any way.

go along with idiom ~에 동조하다, 찬성하다
If you go along with a person or an idea, you agree with them.

joke [dʒouk] n. 농담; 웃음거리; v. 농담하다; 농담 삼아 말하다
A joke is something that is said or done to make you laugh, for example a funny story.

chuckle [tʃʌkl] v. 빙그레 웃다; 킬킬 웃다; n. 속으로 웃기; 킬킬거림
When you chuckle, you laugh quietly.

go on idiom 말을 계속하다; (어떤 상황이) 계속되다; 자자, 어서
If you go on, you continue saying something or talking about something.

practical [prǽktikəl] a. 거의 완전한, 사실상의; 현실적인 (practically ad. 사실상, 거의)
Practically means almost, but not completely or exactly.

saint [seint] n. 성인군자 같은 사람; 성인(聖人) (saintly a. 성자 같은)
If you refer to a living person as a saint, you mean that they are extremely kind, patient, and unselfish.

opposite [ápəzit] n. 반대; a. (정)반대의; 건너편의; 맞은편의
The opposite of someone or something is the person or thing that is most different from them.

black sheep [blæk ʃí:p] idiom (집안·조직의) 골칫덩어리, 말썽꾼
If you describe someone as the black sheep of their family or of a group that they are a member of, you mean that they are considered bad or worthless by other people in that family or group.

be about to idiom 막 ~하려는 참이다
If you are about to do something, you are going to do it immediately.

scratch [skrætʃ] v. (가려운 데를) 긁다; 긁힌 자국을 내다; n. 긁힌 자국; 긁는 소리
If you scratch yourself, you rub your fingernails against your skin because it is itching.

hind [haind] a. 뒤쪽의, 후방의
An animal's hind legs are at the back of its body.

talkative [tɔ́:kətiv] a. 말하기를 좋아하는, 수다스러운
Someone who is talkative talks a lot.

shelter [ʃéltər] n. 보호소; 대피처, 피신처; 피신; v. 막아 주다, 보호하다; 피하다
A shelter is a temporary place to live for people who do not have their
own homes, or for animals who have been treated in a cruel way.

rodent [roudnt] n. (쥐·토끼 등의) 설치류
Rodents are small mammals which have sharp front teeth. Rats, mice,
and squirrels are rodents.

bowl [boul] n. (우묵한) 그릇; 한 그릇(의 양)
A bowl is a round container with a wide uncovered top.

sniff [snif] v. 냄새를 맡다; 코를 훌쩍이다; 콧방귀를 뀌다; n. 냄새 맡기; 콧방귀 뀌기
If you sniff something or sniff at it, you smell it by taking air in through
your nose.

wrinkle [riŋkl] v. (얼굴에) 주름을 잡다, 찡그리다; 주름이 지다; n. 주름
When you wrinkle your nose or forehead, or when it wrinkles, you
tighten the muscles in your face so that the skin folds.

stuff [stʌf] n. 일, 것, 물건; v. 쑤셔 넣다; 채워 넣다
You can use stuff to refer to things such as a substance, a collection of
things, events, or ideas, or the contents of something in a general way
without mentioning the thing itself by name.

by-product [bái-prràdəkt] n. 부산물; 부작용 (meat by-product n. 고기 부산물)
Meat by-products are usable products other than flesh, obtained from
slaughter animals.

pronto [prántou] ad. 빨리, 당장
If you say that something must be done pronto, you mean that it must
be done quickly and at once.

★ **leak** [liːk] n. 소변보기; 틈, 구멍; v. 새게 하다; 새다 (take a leak idiom 소변을 보다)
When someone takes a leak, they get rid of urine from their body.

cranky [krǽŋki] a. 괴팍한; 짜증을 내는; 기이한
Someone who is cranky is not very cheerful and gets angry easily.

복습 **reincarnate** [rìːinkáːrneit] v. 환생시키다 (reincarnated a. 환생한)
If people believe that they will be reincarnated when they die, they believe that their spirit will be born again and will live in the body of another person or animal.

spoil [spɔil] v. 망치다, 버려 놓다; (아이를) 응석받이로 키우다
If you spoil something, you prevent it from being successful or satisfactory.

mood [muːd] n. 기분; 분위기
Your mood is the way you are feeling at a particular time.

Chapter 4

1. **Why was Zack going to visit Grandma Leah?**

   A. To get away from Great-Grandpa Julius

   B. To celebrate a holiday

   C. To help her move

   D. To throw her a surprise party

2. **How did Great-Grandpa Julius convince Zack to bring him to Chicago?**

   A. He promised he would be kind to everyone.

   B. He promised he would not ask for anything else ever again.

   C. He said Grandma Leah was expecting him to come.

   D. He said Grandma Leah would want to see him.

3. **On what condition could Great-Grandpa Julius go to Chicago?**

   A. He could go if he remained quiet during the whole trip.

   B. He could go if he paid for his own flight.

   C. He could go if he spoke to Zack's dad first.

   D. He could go if he got permission from Grandma Leah.

4. **What was Great-Grandpa Julius keeping in a safe place?**

   A. A photo he took with baseball players

   B. Letters he wrote to old baseball players

   C. A baseball signed by famous players

   D. Baseball cards with pictures of top players

5. **What did Zack's dad ask Great-Grandpa Julius?**

   A. He asked about his experience becoming a cat.

   B. He asked for his advice on becoming a cat.

   C. He asked why he was no longer a human.

   D. He asked if he missed being a human.

1분에 몇 단어를 읽는지 리딩 속도를 측정해보세요.

$$\frac{531 \text{ words}}{\text{reading time (} \quad \text{) sec}} \times 60 = (\quad) \text{ WPM}$$

Build Your Vocabulary

deli [déli] n. (= delicatessen) 조제 식품 판매점, 식당
A deli is a delicatessen which is a shop that sells high quality foods such as cheeses and cold meats.

gobble [gabl] v. 게걸스럽게 먹다
If you gobble food, you eat it quickly and greedily.

skimp [skimp] v. (돈·시간 등을) 지나치게 아끼다
If you skimp on something, you use less time, money, or material for it than you really need, so that the result is not good enough.

pushy [púʃi] a. 지나치게 밀어붙이는, 뻔뻔한
If you describe someone as pushy, you mean that they try in a forceful way to get things done as they would like or to increase their status or influence.

★ **allowance** [əláuəns] n. 용돈; 비용, 수당; 허용량
A child's allowance is money that is given to him or her every week or every month by his or her parents.

★ **delighted** [diláitid] a. 아주 기뻐하는 (delightedly ad. 기뻐서)
If you are delighted, you are extremely pleased and excited about something.

복습 **neighbor** [néibər] n. 이웃 (사람); v. 이웃하다, 인접하다
Your neighbor is someone who lives near you.

‡ **crush** [krʌʃ] v. 좌절시키다; 으스러뜨리다; 밀어 넣다; n. 홀딱 반함 (crushed a. 좌절한)
If you are crushed by something, it upsets you a great deal.

‡ **willing** [wíliŋ] a. 기꺼이 ~하는; 자발적인
If someone is willing to do something, they are fairly happy about doing
it and will do it if they are asked or required to do it.

복습 **go along with** idiom ~에 동조하다, 찬성하다
If you go along with a person or an idea, you agree with them.

복습 **joke** [dʒouk] n. 농담; 웃음거리; v. 농담하다; 농담 삼아 말하다
A joke is something that is said or done to make you laugh, for example
a funny story.

복습 **admit** [ædmít] v. 인정하다, 시인하다; 받아들이다
If you admit that something bad, unpleasant, or embarrassing is true,
you agree, often unwillingly, that it is true.

* **tempt** [tempt] v. (좋지 않은 일을 하도록) 유혹하다; 설득하다, 유도하다
(tempted a. ~하고 싶은)
If you say that you are tempted to do something, you mean that you
would like to do it.

복습 **paw** [pɔ:] v. (함부로) 건드리다; 발로 긁다; n. (동물의) 발; (사람의) 손
(paw through idiom 뒤적이다)
If you paw through things, you search through them carelessly or roughly.

* **collection** [kəlékʃən] n. 수집품, 소장품; 무리, 더미; 수집, 수거
A collection of things is a group of similar things that you have
deliberately acquired, usually over a period of time.

fella [félə] n. 남자
You can refer to a man as a fella.

‡ **sign** [sain] v. 서명하다; 신호를 보내다; n. 몸짓, 신호; 표지판; 기색
If you sign, you write your name on something in your own personal way.

복습 **tomcat** [támkæt] n. [동물] 수고양이
A tomcat is a male cat.

nod [nad] v. (고개를) 끄덕이다, 까딱하다; n. (고개를) 끄덕임

If you nod, you move your head downward and upward to show that you are answering 'yes' to a question, or to show agreement, understanding, or approval.

condition [kəndíʃən] n. 조건; 상태; v. 훈련시키다; 좌우하다

When you agree to do something on condition that something else happens, you mean that you will only do it if this other thing also happens.

pad [pæd] v. 소리 안 나게 걷다; 완충재를 대다; n. 패드; (메모지 등의) 묶음

When someone pads somewhere, they walk there with steps that are fairly quick, light, and quiet.

cock [kak] v. 쫑긋 세우다, 높이 들다; 몸을 뒤로 젖히다; n. [동물] 수탉

If you cock a part of your body such as your head or your eyes, you move it upward or in a particular direction.

lock [lak] v. 잠그다; 고정시키다; n. 자물쇠; 잠금장치

When you lock something such as a door, drawer, or case, you fasten it, usually with a key, so that other people cannot open it.

litter [lítər] n. (애완동물의 대소변용) 깔개; 쓰레기; v. 흐트러져 어지럽히다

(litter box n. 애완동물용 변기)

Litter is a dry substance that you put in the container where you want your cat to go to the toilet.

pop [pap] v. 눈이 휘둥그레지다; 불쑥 나타나다; 펑 하는 소리가 나다; n. 펑 (하는 소리)

If your eyes pop, you look very surprised or excited when you see something.

Chapter 5

1. **What did Zack's dad wonder about Great-Grandpa Julius's death?**

   A. He wondered if he had seen a bright light.

   B. He wondered if he had met his old friends.

   C. He wondered if he had gotten stuck in a tunnel.

   D. He wondered if he had had a painful death.

2. **How long had Great-Grandpa Julius been a cat?**

   A. For a few months

   B. For over ten years

   C. Since he retired

   D. Since his human life ended

3. **What was Great-Grandpa Julius's life as a caterpillar like?**

   A. It was pretty stressful.

   B. It was extremely fancy.

   C. It was quite dull.

   D. It was full of surprises.

4. **What happened after Zack, his dad, and Great-Grandpa Julius got on the plane?**

   A. All the passengers stared at Great-Grandpa Julius.

   B. Great-Grandpa Julius jumped out of the cat carrier.

   C. Zack told Great-Grandpa Julius to be silent.

   D. Zack's dad asked Great-Grandpa Julius more questions.

5. **What was true about being a caterpillar, a moth, or a mouse?**

   A. It was harder than being a person.

   B. It could be a very short life.

   C. It involved a lot of responsibility.

   D. It required living with many other creatures.

1분에 몇 단어를 읽는지 리딩 속도를 측정해보세요.

$$\frac{686 \ words}{reading \ time \ (\quad) \ sec} \times 60 = (\quad) \ WPM$$

Build Your Vocabulary

let up idiom 그만두다; 느슨해지다; (강도가) 약해지다, 누그러지다
If you let up, you stop doing something that you have been doing continuously or in a determined way.

ride [raid] n. (차량·자전거 등을) 타고 달리기; 길, 여정; v. (차량·자전거 등을) 타다
A ride is a journey on a horse or bicycle, or in a vehicle.

claim [kleim] v. (~이 사실이라고) 주장하다; 요구하다; n. 청구; 주장
If you say that someone claims that something is true, you mean they say that it is true but you are not sure whether or not they are telling the truth.

tunnel [tʌnl] n. 터널, 굴; v. 터널을 뚫다
A tunnel is a long passage which has been made under the ground, usually through a hill or under the sea.

relative [rélətiv] n. 친척; 동족, 동류; a. 비교적인; 상대적인; 관계가 있는
Your relatives are the members of your family.

bury [béri] v. (땅에) 묻다; 뒤덮다; 감추다
To bury a dead person means to put their body into a grave and cover it with earth.

crave [kreiv] v. 열망하다, 갈망하다; 간절히 원하다
If you crave something, you want to have it very much.

license [láisəns] n. 면허(증); v. (공적으로) 허가하다 (driver's license n. 운전 면허증)
A driver's license is a card showing that you are qualified to drive because you have passed a driving test.

caterpillar [kǽtərpìlər] n. 애벌레
A caterpillar is a small, worm-like animal that feeds on plants and eventually develops into a butterfly or moth.

extreme [ikstríːm] a. 극도의, 극심한; 지나친, 심각한; n. 극단 (extremely ad. 극도로)
You use extremely in front of adjectives and adverbs to emphasize that the specified quality is present to a very great degree.

by any chance idiom 혹시, 혹시라도
You can use by any chance when you are asking questions in order to find out whether something that you think might be true is actually true.

liquor [líkər] n. 술, 독주
Strong alcoholic drinks such as whisky, vodka, and gin can be referred to as liquor.

cab [kæb] n. 택시
A cab is a taxi.

carrier [kǽriər] n. 나르는 것; 항공사, 수송회사; 보균자
Pet carriers are small portable boxes, crates, or cages used to transport small animals such as cats or lap dogs from one location to another.

suitcase [súːtkeis] n. 여행 가방
A suitcase is a box or bag with a handle and a hard frame in which you carry your clothes when you are traveling.

dignify [dígnəfài] v. 품위 있어 보이게 하다; 중요한 것처럼 보이게 하다
(dignified a. 품위 있는)
If you say that someone or something is dignified, you mean they are calm, impressive and deserve respect.

geezer [gíːzər] n. (좀 이상한) 노인; 남자
Some people use geezer to refer to an old man.

★ **sake** [seik] n. 목적; 원인, 이유 (for Pete's sake idiom 도대체, 제발)
Some people use expressions such as 'for God's sake,' 'for heaven's sake,'
or 'for Pete's sake' in order to express annoyance or impatience, or to
add force to a question or request.

‡ **stray** [strei] a. 길을 잃은, 주인이 없는; 빗나간; v. (옳은 길에서) 빗나가다; 길을 잃다
A stray dog or cat has wandered away from its owner's home.

★ **sigh** [sai] v. 한숨을 쉬다, 한숨짓다; 탄식하듯 말하다; n. 한숨
When you sigh, you let out a deep breath, as a way of expressing feelings
such as disappointment, tiredness, or pleasure.

‡ **moth** [mɔːθ] n. 나방
A moth is an insect like a butterfly which usually flies about at night.

‡ **knock** [nak] v. 비판하다; (문 등을) 두드리다; 치다; n. 문 두드리는 소리; 부딪침
If you knock something or someone, you criticize them and say
unpleasant things about them.

tasty [téisti] a. 맛있는
If you say that food, especially savory food, is tasty, you mean that it has
a fairly strong and pleasant flavor which makes it good to eat.

rye [rai] n. 호밀빵; 호밀
Rye is bread made from rye grain.

★ **torch** [tɔːrʃ] n. 횃불
A torch is a long stick with burning material at one end, used to provide
light or to set things on fire.

‡ **suppose** [səpóuz] v. ～인 것 같다; 생각하다, 추측하다
You can say 'I suppose' when you want to express slight uncertainty.

do a stretch idiom (교도소에서) 형기를 살다
If you do a stretch in prison, you spend a period of time in prison.

matter [mǽtər] v. 중요하다; 문제되다; n. 문제, 일; 상황, 사태; 물질
If you say that something does not matter, you mean that it is not important to you because it does not have an effect on you or on a particular situation.

leisure [líːʒər] a. 한가한, 여가의; n. 여가 (leisure time n. 여가 시간)
Leisure time is the time when you are not working and you can relax and do things that you enjoy.

flight [flait] n. 비행; 항공기; 계단
A flight is a journey made by flying, usually in an airplane.

attendant [əténdənt] n. 안내원, 수행원; 참석자 (flight attendant n. 승무원)
On an airplane, the flight attendants are the people whose job is to look after the passengers and serve their meals.

row [rou] n. 열, 줄; 노 젓기; v. 노를 젓다
A row of things or people is a number of them arranged in a line.

takeoff [téikɔ̀ːf] n. 이륙, 도약; 제거, 분리
Takeoff is the beginning of a flight, when an aircraft leaves the ground.

secure [sikjúər] a. 단단한; 안전한; 안심하는; v. (단단히) 고정시키다; 얻어 내다
(securely ad. 단단히)
If an object is secure, it is fixed firmly in position.

fasten [fǽsn] v. 매다, 채우다; (단단히) 잠그다; 고정시키다
When you fasten something, you close it by means of buttons or a strap, or some other device.

tray [trei] n. 쟁반 (tray table n. 쟁반 같은 탁자)
A tray is a flat piece of wood, plastic, or metal, which usually has raised edges and which is used for carrying things, especially food and drinks.

upright [Ápràit] a. 수직으로 세워 둔; (자세가) 똑바른
Something that is upright stands straight up.

^복_습 **lock** [lak] v. 고정시키다; 잠그다; n. 자물쇠; 잠금장치

If you lock something in a particular position or if it locks there, it is held or fitted firmly in that position.

give a dirty look idiom ~를 째려 보다

If you give someone a dirty look, you look at them in an angry or a disapproving way.

★ **buckle** [bʌkl] v. 버클로 잠그다; 찌그러지다; n. 버클, 잠금장치
(buckle up idiom 안전벨트를 매다)

If you buckle up, you to fasten the belt that keeps you in your seat in a car or a plane.

Chapter
6

1. **What happened when Zack told Grandma Leah that the cat was her father?**

    A. She was too stunned to reply.

    B. She got really emotional.

    C. She simply denied it.

    D. She felt very offended.

2. **Why wouldn't Grandma Leah speak directly to the cat?**

    A. She did not have conversations with cats.

    B. She disliked animals that could talk.

    C. She was too nervous to talk to the cat.

    D. She could not understand the cat's responses.

3. **How did the cat act in Grandma Leah's home?**
   A. He spoke in a relaxed way.
   B. He tried to look adorable.
   C. He acted like he did not care.
   D. He seemed to be getting impatient.

4. **According to the cat, why couldn't he remember what Grandma Leah called her father?**
   A. All of his memories got erased when he died.
   B. His memory was not that strong anymore.
   C. He had been called many names when he was alive.
   D. He had never spent much time with Grandma Leah.

5. **How did Grandma Leah figure out who the cat was?**
   A. She realized the cat looked like Great-Grandpa Maurice.
   B. She noticed the cat's voice sounded like Great-Grandpa Maurice's.
   C. Her father had never done things that the cat wanted to do.
   D. The cat finally gave up and revealed his real name.

1분에 몇 단어를 읽는지 리딩 속도를 측정해보세요.

$$\frac{824 \text{ words}}{\text{reading time (} \quad \text{) sec}} \times 60 = (\quad) \text{ WPM}$$

Build Your Vocabulary

shore [ʃɔ:r] n. 해안, 해변, 호숫가
The shores or the shore of a sea, lake, or wide river is the land along the edge of it.

peppy [pépi] a. 기운이 넘치는, 활발한
Someone or something that is peppy is lively and full of energy.

open-minded [oupən-máindid] a. 마음이 열린, 편견 없는
If you describe someone as open-minded, you approve of them because they are willing to listen to and consider other people's ideas and suggestions.

hall [hɔ:l] n. 복도; 현관; 넓은 방
A hall in a building is a long passage with doors into rooms on both sides of it.

luggage [lʌ́gidʒ] n. (여행용) 짐
Luggage is the suitcases and bags that you take with you when travel.

settle [setl] v. 편하게 앉다; 자리를 잡다; 결정하다
If you settle yourself somewhere or settle somewhere, you sit down or make yourself comfortable.

notice [nóutis] v. 알아채다, 인지하다; 주의하다; n. 신경 씀, 알아챔; 통지, 예고
If you notice something or someone, you become aware of them.

in other words idiom 다시 말해서
You say 'in other words' in order to introduce a different, and usually simpler, explanation or interpretation of something that has just been said.

stare [stɛər] v. 빤히 쳐다보다, 응시하다; n. 빤히 쳐다보기, 응시
If you stare at someone or something, you look at them for a long time.

dear [diər] n. 아가, 여보; a. 사랑하는, 소중한; ~에게; int. 이런
You can call someone dear as a sign of affection.

darling [dáːrliŋ] n. 자기, 얘야; a. (대단히) 사랑하는; 굉장히 멋진
You call someone darling if you love them or like them very much.

deaf [def] a. 귀가 먹은, 청각 장애가 있는; ~에 귀를 기울이지 않는
Someone who is deaf is unable to hear anything or is unable to hear very well.

soften [sɔ́ːfən] v. (비판·노여움 등이) 누그러지다, 누그러뜨리다; 부드러워지다
If your voice or expression softens or if you soften it, it becomes much more gentle and friendly.

snap [snæp] v. 날카롭게 말하다; 급히 움직이다; 툭 부러지다; n. 탁 하는 소리
If someone snaps at you, they speak to you in a sharp, unfriendly way.

recover [rikʌ́vər] v. 되찾다, 회복하다; 회복되다; (손실 등을) 되찾다
If you recover a mental or physical state, it comes back again.

composure [kəmpóuʒər] n. (마음의) 평정
Composure is the appearance or feeling of calm and the ability to control your feelings.

caterpillar [kǽtərpìlər] n. 애벌레
A caterpillar is a small, worm-like animal that feeds on plants and eventually develops into a butterfly or moth.

moth [mɔːθ] n. 나방
A moth is an insect like a butterfly which usually flies about at night.

give a break idiom ~를 너그럽게 봐주다; ~에게 기회를 주다
If you give someone a break, you stop criticizing them or being angry
with them.

go on idiom 자자, 어서; 말을 계속하다; (어떤 상황이) 계속되다
You can use 'go on' to encourage someone to do something.

wave [weiv] v. (손이나 팔을) 흔들다; 손짓하다; n. 물결; (손이나 팔을) 흔들기
If you wave or wave your hand, you move your hand from side to side
in the air, usually in order to say hello or goodbye to someone.

paw [pɔː] n. (동물의) 발; (사람의) 손; v. 발로 긁다; (함부로) 건드리다
The paws of an animal such as a cat, dog, or bear are its feet, which have
claws for gripping things and soft pads for walking on.

dismissive [dismísiv] a. 무시하는, 멸시하는; 거만한 (dismissively ad. 무시하듯)
If you are dismissive of someone or something, you say or show that you
think they are not important or have no value.

far from idiom 전혀 ~이 아닌, ~와는 거리가 먼
If you say that something is far from a particular thing, you are
emphasizing that it is not that particular thing, especially when people
expect or assume that it is.

realize [ríːəlàiz] v. 깨닫다, 알아차리다; 실현하다, 달성하다
If you realize that something is true, you become aware of that fact or
understand it.

black sheep [blæk ʃíːp] n. (집안·조직의) 골칫덩어리, 말썽꾼
If you describe someone as the black sheep of their family or of a group
that they are a member of, you mean that they are considered bad or
worthless by other people in that family or group.

no-good [nóu-gud] a. 쓸모없는; 못된
A no-good person does nothing useful or helpful and is therefore
considered to be of little value.

Chapter 7

1. **Why was Grandma Leah mad at Great-Grandpa Maurice?**

   A. He ruined her father's reputation in town.

   B. He destroyed the neighborhood with his inventions.

   C. He did crazy experiments on their family.

   D. He did not return money that he owed.

2. **What kind of things did Great-Grandpa Maurice invent?**

   A. Things that already existed

   B. Things that would improve people's lives

   C. Things for different animals

   D. Things for young children

3. **How did Great-Grandpa Maurice earn all the money back?**

   A. He designed clothing for people who love dogs.

   B. He designed a sweater with a hot dog on it.

   C. He sold hot dogs at a famous hot dog stand.

   D. He sold a dog sweater that became popular.

4. **What did Great-Grandpa Maurice do before he died?**

   A. He applied for a loan at a bank in Chicago.

   B. He transferred money to a Chicago bank account.

   C. He opened a secret bank account with Great-Grandpa Julius.

   D. He took all of his cash with him on a bus.

5. **What did Zack think of Great-Grandpa Maurice's story?**

   A. It proved that Great-Grandpa Maurice could be trusted.

   B. It showed that Great-Grandpa Maurice was a good person.

   C. It was not something that should be automatically believed.

   D. There was no way that it could be false.

1분에 몇 단어를 읽는지 리딩 속도를 측정해보세요.

$$\frac{370 \text{ words}}{\text{reading time (} \quad \text{) sec}} \times 60 = (\quad) \text{ WPM}$$

Build Your Vocabulary

demand [dimǽnd] v. 강력히 묻다, 따지다; 요구하다; n. 요구; 수요
If you demand something such as information or action, you ask for it in a very forceful way.

tomcat [támkæt] n. [동물] 수고양이
A tomcat is a male cat.

no-good [nóu-gud] a. 쓸모없는; 못된
A no-good person does nothing useful or helpful and is therefore considered to be of little value.

hold one's horses idiom 침착하다, 참다, 서두르지 않다
You can say 'hold your horses' to someone to tell them to stop and consider carefully their decision or opinion about something.

get off idiom 뻔뻔하게도 ~하다; 출발하다
(where does someone get off idiom 무슨 권리로 ~하는 거야?)
You can use 'where does someone get off doing something' for saying that you think they are wrong to behave in a particular way.

work on idiom (해결·개선하기 위해) ~에 애쓰다
If you work on something, you spend time producing or improving it.

invent [invént] v. 발명하다; (사실이 아닌 것을) 지어내다 (invention n. 발명품)
An invention is a machine, tool, or system that someone has made, designed, or thought of for the first time.

‡ **disappear** [dìsəpíər] v. 없어지다; 사라지다, 보이지 않게 되다
If someone or something disappears, they go away or are taken away
somewhere where nobody can find them.

hairpiece [hέərpi:s] n. 부분 가발
A hairpiece is a piece of false hair that some people wear on their head
if they are bald or if they want to make their own hair seem longer or
thicker.

⋆ **bald** [bɔ:ld] a. 대머리의, 머리가 벗겨진
Someone who is bald has little or no hair on the top of their head.

‡ **whistle** [hwisl] n. 호루라기; 휘파람; 기적, 경적; v. 휘파람을 불다; 기적을 울리다
A whistle is a small metal tube which you blow in order to produce a
loud sound and attract someone's attention.

복습 **go on** idiom 말을 계속하다; (어떤 상황이) 계속되다; 자자, 어서
If you go on, you continue saying something or talking about something.

be supposed to idiom ~하기로 되어 있다, ~해야 한다
If you say that something is supposed to happen, you mean that it is
planned or expected.

‡ **except** [iksépt] prep. ~을 제외하고는, ~외에는; v. 제외하다
You use except for to introduce the only thing or person that prevents
a statement from being completely true.

‡ **embarrass** [imbǽrəs] v. 당황스럽게 하다, 어색하게 하다; 곤란하게 하다
(embarrassed a. 당황스러운, 어색한)
A person who is embarrassed feels shy, ashamed, or guilty about
something.

⋆ **blow** [blou] v. (blew–blown) (악기 등을) 불다; (바람이) 불다; n. 강타; 충격
When a whistle or horn blows or someone blows it, they make a sound
by blowing into it.

복습 **neighbor** [néibər] n. 이웃 (사람); v. 이웃하다, 인접하다 (neighborhood n. 근처, 인근)
The neighborhood of a place or person is the area or the people around
them.

bun [bʌn] n. (둥근) 빵
A bun is a small, round piece of bread.

beat it idiom 떠나다; 저리 가!
If you beat it, you leave immediately.

⁑ **account** [əkáunt] n. 계좌; 설명, 이야기; v. 간주하다, 여기다
If you have an account with a bank or a similar organization, you have
an arrangement to leave your money there and take some out when
you need it.

⁑ **loan** [loun] n. 대출; 대여; v. 빌려주다, 대여하다
A loan is a sum of money that you borrow.

⁑ **association** [əsòusiéiʃən] n. 협회; 유대, 제휴; 연관
An association is an official group of people who have the same job,
aim, or interest.

복습 **stare** [stɛər] v. 빤히 쳐다보다, 응시하다; n. 빤히 쳐다보기, 응시
If you stare at someone or something, you look at them for a long time.

Chapter 8

1. What was the problem at the bank?

   A. Great-Grandpa Maurice could not remember his account number.

   B. Great-Grandpa Maurice's signature was needed.

   C. The name on the account was not Great-Grandpa Maurice's.

   D. Someone had closed Great-Grandpa Maurice's account a long time ago.

2. Who was Morty?

   A. The person who established the bank

   B. The new president of the bank

   C. Great-Grandpa Maurice's best friend

   D. Great Grandpa Maurice's lawyer

3. **What was true about Morty?**
   A. He had never met Great-Grandpa Maurice before.
   B. He knew Great-Grandpa Maurice would visit.
   C. He had poor eyesight.
   D. He was quite young.

4. **What did Morty think about Great-Grandpa Maurice's situation?**
   A. It was odd that Great-Grandpa Maurice wanted to withdraw his money.
   B. It was unreasonable to give Great-Grandpa Maurice money when he was a cat.
   C. Great-Grandpa Maurice forgot how to hold a pen because he was a cat.
   D. Great-Grandpa Maurice could not sign by himself because he was old.

5. **What did Great-Grandpa Maurice want to do with part of the money?**
   A. He wanted to move to Florida.
   B. He wanted to open a pet hotel.
   C. He wanted to travel around the world.
   D. He wanted to learn how to cook herring and sour cream.

1분에 몇 단어를 읽는지 리딩 속도를 측정해보세요.

$$\frac{1,545 \text{ words}}{\text{reading time (\quad) sec}} \times 60 = (\quad) \text{ WPM}$$

Build Your Vocabulary

cab [kæb] n. 택시
A cab is a taxi.

loan [loun] n. 대출; 대여; v. 빌려주다, 대여하다
A loan is a sum of money that you borrow.

association [əsòusiéiʃən] n. 협회; 유대, 제휴; 연관
An association is an official group of people who have the same job, aim, or interest.

officer [ɔ́:fisər] n. 직원; 경찰관; 장교; 공무원
An officer is a person who has a responsible position in an organization or the government.

account [əkáunt] n. 계좌; 설명, 이야기; v. 간주하다, 여기다
If you have an account with a bank or a similar organization, you have an arrangement to leave your money there and take some out when you need it.

bear [bɛər] v. (특정한 이름을) 가지다, 지니다; 참다, 견디다; (아이를) 낳다; n. [동물] 곰
If something bears a particular mark or characteristic, it has that mark or characteristic.

carrier [kǽriər] n. 나르는 것; 항공사, 수송회사; 보균자
Pet carriers are small portable boxes, crates, or cages used to transport small animals such as cats or lap dogs from one location to another.

* **startle** [stá:rtl] v. 깜짝 놀라게 하다; 움찔하다; n. 깜짝 놀람 (startled a. 놀란)
If something sudden and unexpected startles you, it surprises and frightens you slightly.

mistrust [mistrʌ́st] v. 신뢰하지 않다; n. 불신 (mistrustful a. 의심 많은)
If you are mistrustful of someone, you do not trust them.

복습 **nod** [nad] v. (고개를) 끄덕이다, 까딱하다; n. (고개를) 끄덕임
If you nod, you move your head downward and upward to show that you are answering 'yes' to a question, or to show agreement, understanding, or approval.

‡ **individual** [ìndəvídʒuəl] n. 개인; a. 각각의; 개인의; 개성 있는
An individual is a person.

복습 **sign** [sain] v. 서명하다; 신호를 보내다; n. 몸짓, 신호; 표지판; 기색
When you sign a document, you write your name on it, usually at the end or in a special space.

decease [disí:s] v. 사망하다; n. 사망 (deceased a. 사망한)
A deceased person is one who has recently died.

probate [próubeit] n. (유언장에 대한) 공증; v. (유언장을) 공증하다
Probate is the act or process of officially proving a will to be valid.

* **complicate** [kámpləkèit] v. 복잡하게 하다; 곤란하게 하다 (complicated a. 복잡한)
If you say that something is complicated, you mean it has so many parts or aspects that it is difficult to understand or deal with.

‡ **legal** [lí:gəl] a. 법률과 관련된; 법이 허용하는, 합법적인
Legal is used to describe things that relate to the law.

‡ **process** [práses] n. 과정, 절차; 공정; v. (공식적으로) 처리하다; 가공하다
A process is a series of actions which are carried out in order to achieve a particular result.

sort out idiom ~을 처리하다; ~을 정리하다
If you sort out something, you do what is necessary to deal with a problem, disagreement, or difficult situation successfully.

★ **whisper** [hwíspər] v. 소곤거리다, 속삭이다; n. 소곤거리는 소리, 속삭임
When you whisper, you say something very quietly, using your breath
rather than your throat, so that only one person can hear you.

turn into idiom ~이 되다, ~으로 변하다
To turn into means to change or develop into something different.

복습 **reincarnate** [rìːinkáːrneit] v. 환생시키다 (reincarnation n. 환생)
If you believe in reincarnation, you believe that you will be born again
and will live in the body of another person or animal after you die.

★ **alarm** [əláːrm] v. 불안하게 하다; 경보장치를 달다; n. 불안, 공포; 경보 장치
(alarmed a. 불안해하는)
If someone is alarmed, they feel afraid or anxious that something
unpleasant or dangerous might happen.

★ **shrug** [ʃrʌg] v. (어깨를) 으쓱하다; n. 어깨를 으쓱하기
If you shrug, you raise your shoulders to show that you are not interested
in something or that you do not know or care about something.

★ **hop** [hap] v. 깡충깡충 뛰다; 급히 움직이다; n. 깡충깡충 뛰기
When birds and some small animals hop, they move along by jumping
on both feet.

★ **counter** [káuntər] n. 계산대; 판매대; 반대, 반작용; v. 반박하다; 대응하다
In a place such as a shop or café a counter is a long narrow table or flat
surface at which customers are served.

복습 **pet** [pet] n. 애완동물; v. (다정하게) 어루만지다
A pet is an animal that you keep in your home to give you company
and pleasure.

★ **regulate** [régjulèit] v. 규제하다; (기계 등을) 조절하다 (regulation n. 규정)
Regulations are rules made by a government or other authority in order
to control the way something is done or the way people behave.

복습 **specific** [spisífik] a. 구체적인, 분명한; 특정한 (specifically ad. 분명히, 명확하게)
You use specifically to emphasize that something is given special
attention and considered separately from other things of the same kind.

forbid [fərbíd] v. 금하다; ~을 어렵게 하다
If you forbid someone to do something, or if you forbid an activity, you order that it must not be done.

pipe down idiom 조용히 해, 입 다물어
You can use 'pipe down' to someone for telling them to stop talking or to make less noise.

clear up idiom ~을 해결하다, 설명하다
If you clear up something, you explain or solve it, or make it easier to understand.

faint [feint] v. 실신하다, 기절하다; n. 실신, 기절; a. 희미한, 약한
If you faint, you lose consciousness for a short time, especially because you are hungry, or because of pain, heat, or shock.

lean [liːn] v. ~에 기대다; 기울이다, (몸을) 숙이다; a. 군살이 없는, 호리호리한
If you lean on or against someone or something, you rest against them so that they partly support your weight.

withdraw [wiðdrɔ́ː] v. (계좌에서 돈을) 인출하다; 물러나다
If you withdraw money from a bank account, you take it out of that account.

barely [béərli] ad. 간신히, 가까스로; 거의 ~아니게
You use barely to say that something is only just true or only just the case.

notice [nóutis] v. 알아채다, 인지하다; 주의하다; n. 신경 씀, 알아챔; 통지, 예고
If you notice something or someone, you become aware of them.

opposable [əpóuzəbl] a. 마주 볼 수 있는; 적대할 수 있는
Opposable thumbs are thumbs that can be put opposite the fingers of the same hand, so that objects can be picked up and held.

thumb [θʌm] n. 엄지손가락; v. 엄지손가락으로 건드리다
Your thumb is the short thick part on the side of your hand next to your four fingers.

⁎ **consistent** [kənsístənt] a. ~와 일치하는; 일관된
If one fact or idea is consistent with another, they do not contradict
each other.

⁎ **policy** [páləsi] n. 정책, 방침; 보험 증권
A policy is a set of ideas or plans that is used as a basis for making
decisions, especially in politics, economics, or business.

⁎ **squeeze** [skwiːz] v. (눈을 꼭) 감다; 짜다; (좁은 곳에) 비집고 들어가다; n. 쥐기
If your eyes squeeze shut, you close them tightly.

⁎ **found** [faund] v. 설립하다; 세우다, 만들다; ~에 기초를 두다 (founder n. 설립자, 창립자)
The founder of an institution, organization, or building is the person who
got it started or caused it to be built, often by providing the necessary
money.

⁎ **leap** [liːp] v. (leapt–leapt) 뛰다, 뛰어오르다; (서둘러) ~하다; n. 높이뛰기, 도약; 급증
If you leap, you jump high in the air or jump a long distance.

hotfoot it idiom 부리나케 가다, 서둘러 가다
If you hotfoot it, you go somewhere fast and in a hurry.

복습 **hall** [hɔːl] n. 복도; 현관; 넓은 방
A hall in a building is a long passage with doors into rooms on both
sides of it.

복습 **fancy** [fǽnsi] a. 화려한, 장식이 많은; 고급의; 복잡한; v. 생각하다, 상상하다
If you describe something as fancy, you mean that it is special, unusual,
or elaborate, for example because it has a lot of decoration.

⁎ **yell** [jel] v. 고함치다, 소리 지르다; n. 고함, 외침
If you yell, you shout loudly, usually because you are excited, angry, or
in pain.

⁎ **antique** [æntíːk] n. 골동품; a. (귀중한) 골동품인
An antique is an old object such as a piece of china or furniture which
is valuable because of its beauty or rarity.

doubt [daut] v. 확신하지 못하다, 의심하다, 의문을 갖다; n. 의심, 의혹, 의문

If you doubt whether something is true or possible, you believe that it is probably not true or possible.

amaze [əméiz] v. (대단히) 놀라게 하다; 경악하게 하다 (amazingly ad. 놀랄 만큼)

You say that something is amazing when it is very surprising and makes you feel pleasure, approval, or wonder.

squint [skwint] v. 눈을 가늘게 뜨고 보다; 사시이다; n. 사시; 잠깐 봄

If you squint at something, you look at it with your eyes partly closed.

peer [piər] v. 유심히 보다, 눈여겨보다; n. 또래

If you peer at something, you look at it very hard, usually because it is difficult to see clearly.

recognize [rékəgnàiz] v. 알아보다; 인식하다; 공인하다

If you recognize someone or something, you know who that person is or what that thing is.

never mind idiom 신경 쓰지 마

You use 'never mind' to tell someone that they need not do something or worry about something, because it is not important or because you will do it yourself.

realize [ríːəlàiz] v. 깨닫다, 알아차리다; 실현하다, 달성하다

If you realize that something is true, you become aware of that fact or understand it.

snap [snæp] v. 날카롭게 말하다; 급히 움직이다; 툭 부러지다; n. 탁 하는 소리

If someone snaps at you, they speak to you in a sharp, unfriendly way.

poppycock [pápikòk] n. 허튼 소리, 실없는 소리

You can use poppycock to refer to something that you think is foolish or that you disapprove of.

roar [rɔːr] v. 고함치다; 으르렁거리다; n. 함성; 울부짖는 듯한 소리

If someone roars, they shout something in a very loud voice.

★ **invest** [invést] v. 투자하다; (권력·권한 등을) 부여하다
If you invest in something, or if you invest a sum of money, you use your money in a way that you hope will increase its value, for example by paying it into a bank, or buying shares or property.

복습 **paw** [pɔː] n. (동물의) 발; (사람의) 손; v. 발로 긁다; (함부로) 건드리다
The paws of an animal such as a cat, dog, or bear are its feet, which have claws for gripping things and soft pads for walking on.

복습 **dear** [diər] n. 아가, 여보; int. 이런; a. 사랑하는, 소중한; ～에게
You can call someone dear as a sign of affection.

복습 **whistle** [hwisl] v. 휘파람을 불다; 기적을 울리다; n. 호루라기; 휘파람; 기적, 경적
When someone whistles, they make a sound by forcing their breath out between their lips or their teeth.

복습 **interest** [íntərəst] n. 이자, 이율; 흥미; 이익; v. 관심을 끌다
Interest is extra money that you receive if you have invested a sum of money.

복습 **condition** [kəndíʃən] n. 조건; 상태; v. 훈련시키다; 좌우하다
When you agree to do something on condition that something else happens, you mean that you will only do it if this other thing also happens.

★ **rent** [rent] n. 집세, 방세; v. 빌리다
Rent is the amount of money that you pay regularly to use a house, flat, or piece of land.

deluxe [dəlʌ́ks] a. 고급의
Deluxe goods or services are better in quality and more expensive than ordinary ones.

standing order [stǽndiŋ ɔ́ːrdər] n. 정기 주문; 자동 이체
A standing order is an arrangement in which goods are sent regularly in agreed amounts, without the customer having to make a new order each time.

golden years [góuldən jiərz] n. 노후
Golden years refer to the years that follow retirement from work.

folk [fouk] n. (pl.) 사람들; 여러분, 얘들아; 가족, 부모; a. 민속의, 전통적인
You can refer to people as folk or folks.

willing [wíliŋ] a. 기꺼이 ~하는; 자발적인
If someone is willing to do something, they are fairly happy about doing it and will do it if they are asked or required to do it.

invent [invént] v. 발명하다; (사실이 아닌 것을) 지어내다 (invention n. 발명품)
An invention is a machine, tool, or system that someone has made, designed, or thought of for the first time.

speculate [spékjulèit] v. 투기하다; 추측하다, 짐작하다 (speculative a. 투기적인)
Speculative is used to describe activities which involve buying goods or shares, or buildings and properties, in the hope of being able to sell them again at a higher price and make a profit.

nature [néitʃər] n. 종류, 유형; 본질; 자연
The nature of something is its basic quality or character.

deposit [dipázit] n. 보관; 보증금; 예금; v. (특정한 곳에) 두다; 예금하다
The deposit is the action of placing something in a specified place for safekeeping.

pussycat [púsikæt] n. 야옹이, 고양이; (예상외로) 친근한 사람
Children or people talking to children often refer to a cat as a pussycat.

pushy [púʃi] a. 지나치게 밀어붙이는, 뻔뻔한
If you describe someone as pushy, you mean that they try in a forceful way to get things done as they would like or to increase their status or influence.

cheer up idiom 기운을 내다; ~을 격려하다
If someone cheers up, or something cheers someone up, they start to feel happier.

shelter [ʃéltər] n. 대피처, 피신처; 피신; v. 막아 주다, 보호하다; 피하다
A shelter is a temporary place to live for people who do not have their own homes, or for animals who have been treated in a cruel way.

kitten [kitn] n. [동물] 새끼 고양이
A kitten is a very young cat.

flea [fliː] n. 벼룩
A flea is a very small jumping insect that has no wings and feeds on the blood of humans or animals.

worm [wəːrm] n. 기생충; (땅 속에 사는) 벌레; v. 꿈틀거리며 나아가다
If animals or people have worms, worms are living in their intestines.

litter [lítər] n. (애완동물의 대소변용) 깔개; 쓰레기; v. 흐트러져 어지럽히다
(litter box n. 애완동물용 변기)
Litter is a dry substance that you put in the container where you want your cat to go to the toilet.

★ **overlook** [òuvərlúk] v. 눈감아주다; 바라보다, 내려다보다; n. 전망이 좋은 곳
If you overlook someone's faults or bad behavior, you forgive them and take no action.

former [fɔ́ːrmər] a. 이전의, 과거의; 옛날의; 전자의
Former is used to describe a situation or period of time which came before the present one.

1장

제 이름은 잭(Zack)입니다. 저는 열 살이고 제 평생 기이한 것들에 관심을 가져 왔다고 말할 수 있을 것입니다. 귀신이 나오는 집, UFO, 그리고 개구리들이 쏟아져 내리는 폭풍우 같은 것에 말이에요. 그렇기 때문에 저는 어떤 기이한 일이 저에게 일어났을 때, 평생 기이한 것에 관심을 두지 않았던 다른 사람들보다 아마도 더 마음이 열려 있었던 것 같습니다.

저는 뉴욕시의 우리집 근처에 있는 동물 보호소에 있었습니다. 몇 년이나 아빠에게 고양이를 기르게 해 달라고 간청한 후, 아빠는 드디어 항복했고 그렇게 하자고 말했습니다. 저는 새끼 고양이를 가질 수 있었습니다. 그래서 제가 이곳에 있게 되었죠.

저는 늙은 회색 수고양이가 들어 있는 우리를 지나쳤습니다. 그의 털에는 먼지가 엉겨붙어 있었습니다. 그는 그의 얼굴 왼쪽에 있는 수염의 절반을 잃었고, 그것이 그를 한쪽이 약간 처진 것처럼 보이게 했습니다. 그리고 그의 한쪽 귀의 끝은 물어 뜯겨 있었습니다.

"쉬이이! 얘야!" 누군가가 저를 불렀습니다. 그 목소리는 거칠고 이상하게 들렸습니다. "안녕, 꼬마야! 여기야!"

그게 누구였는지 보려고, 저는 돌아섰습니다. 하지만 아무도 보이지 않았습니다.

저는 몸은 까맣고 발은 하얀색인 작은 턱시도(tuxedo) 새끼 고양이가 낮잠을 자고 있는 우리 쪽으로 계속 나아갔습니다. 그는 확실히 귀여웠습니다. 저는 그를 더 자세히 보기 위해 멈춰 섰습니다. 물론, 어쩌면 제가 고양이를 입양하기에 가장 좋은 시기는 아니었을지도 모릅니다. 이틀 후에 아빠와 저는 레아 할머니(Grandma Leah)와 추수감사절을 보내기 위해 비행기를 타고 시카고(Chicago)로 갈 것이었습니다. 하지만 우리의 이웃이 고양이를 봐 주기로 했습니다. 그리고 저는 아빠가 마음을 바꿀 위험을 감수하고 싶지 않았습니다.

제가 그 작고 귀여운 턱시도 고양이를 데려가기로 거의 결정했을 때 저는 다시 목소리를 들었습니다:

"어이, 얘야." 목소리가 말했습니다. "내가 지금 너에게 *말하고 있잖니.*"

"어디에 있어?" 제가 물었습니다.

"바로 여기다, 바보야." 목소리가 말했습니다. "네 뒤에 있는 우리 안이야."

저는 돌아섰습니다. 그 꾀죄죄한 늙은 회색 수고양이가 꽤나 짜증이 난 채로 저를 바라보고 있었습니다.

"소리친 건 용서해 줘." 고양이가 말했습니다. "하지만 나는 네가 끔찍한 실수를 해서 다른 고양이를 선택하게 될까

봐 걱정됐어.”

“너 말할 수 있구나!” 제가 듣고 있는 게 진짜인지 거의 믿을 수 없어서, 저는 말했습니다.

저는 그의 우리로 더 가까이 다가섰습니다. 저는 그가 말할 때 그의 고양이 입술이 움직이는지 보고 싶었습니다. 아마 이것은 단지 속임수에 불과할지도 모릅니다—누군가 복화술을 하는 것일지도 몰라요. 제가 기이한 것을 좋아한다고 말하기는 했지만, 이건 정말로 극단적인 일이었어요, 심지어 저에게도요. “말하는 고양이라고?” 제가 말했습니다.

“그래, 말하는 고양이, 바로 그거야.” 고양이가 비꼬듯이 말했습니다.

그의 고양이 입술이 움직이고 있었습니다! 이건 속임수가 아니었어요!

“하지만 봐라—너는 말하는 소년이잖니.” 그가 말했습니다. “들어 봐, 우리에게는 시간이 많이 없어. 네가 나를 여기에서 내보내 줘야 해.”

“무슨 뜻이야?”

“내가 이곳에 있는 것을 1분도 더 참을 수가 없다는 말이야.” 그가 말했습니다. “야옹야옹 우는 소리와 냄새가 나를 미치게 하고 있어. 저들에게 네가 나를 입양할 거라고 말해.”

“어, 네 감정을 상하게 할 생각은 아닌데.” 제가 말했습니다. “그렇지만 나는

벌써 여기 이 작은 턱시도 새끼 고양이를 데려가기로 결정했어.” 제가 전에 말했듯이, 저는 꽤 마음이 열려 있습니다. 저는 말하는 고양이에 대해 나쁜 감정은 없었습니다. 그저 그것과 함께 살고 싶은지에 대해 확신할 수 없었죠. 특히 이 고양이가 그러는 것처럼 으스대는 고양이와 함께 말입니다.

“그 턱시도 새끼 고양이?” 그가 말했습니다. “형편없는 선택이야.”

“무슨 뜻이야?”

“그에게는 벼룩과 기생충이 있어. 게다가 그는 고양이 화장실을 전혀 사용할 줄 몰라.”

고양이는 저를 오랫동안 살펴봤습니다. 그는 제가 그 말을 믿지 않는다는 걸 알 수 있었습니다.

“좋아.” 고양이가 계속 말했습니다. “이 방법까지는 쓰지 않으려고 했는데. 하지만 들어 봐: 네가 나를 입양하지 않으면, 그들이 나를 잠들게 할 거야. 그리고 이건 내 잠옷을 입혀서 나를 잠자리에 들게 한다는 뜻이 아니야. 나를 죽인다는 말이야. 네 양심을 걸고 너는 정말로 그걸 원하니, 애야?”

“있지, 그들은 여기에서 고양이를 안락사시키지 않아.” 제가 말했습니다. “그건 아주 잘 알려진 사실이야.” 이 고양이는 으스댈 뿐만 아니라, 진실을 말하는 일에 대해서도 문제가 좀 있는 것처

럼 보였습니다.

"좋아. 나도 그들이 최근에는 그러지 않았다는 걸 인정해." 그가 말했습니다. "하지만 그건 언제라도 바뀔 수 있어."

저는 그를 바라보았고 고개를 저었습니다.

"알았어, 알았어." 그가 말했습니다. "그럼 이건 어떨까: 내가 너에게 네 이름을 알고 있다고 말한다면?"

"내 이름이 뭔데?"

"잭."

"어떻게—어떻게 그걸 알았어?" 제가 물었습니다. 저는 제가 꽤 감명받았다는 걸 인정해야 했습니다. 제 이름을 아는 사람은 그렇게 많지 않고, 심지어 그런 고양이는 훨씬 더 적었습니다.

"너 감명받았구나, 응?" 커다란 회색 수고양이가 말했습니다. "만약 내가 너에게 내가 네 가족의 일원이라고 말한다면, 잭? 그래도 네가 여전히 저 작은 턱시도 고양이를 더 좋아할 것 같니?"

"내 *가족의 일원*이라고?" 제가 말했습니다. "어떻게 그럴 수가 있어? 너는 고양이잖아."

"얘, 너는 환생에 대해서 들어 본 적이 없니? 어떤 사람이 죽고 나서 다른 사람으로 다시 돌아오는 것 말이야?"

"그래서?" 제가 말했습니다. 확실히, 저는 환생에 대해 들어 본 적이 있습니다. 사실, 저는 전생을 살았다고 주장

하는 아이들에 대한 인도에서 있었던 몇 가지 사례에 대해 읽어 본 적이 있습니다. 그들은 한 번도 가 본 적이 없는 어떤 장소에 대한 사실이나, 그들이 평범한 아이라면 도저히 알 수 없는 것들에 대해 알고 있었습니다. 그렇다고 해도, 그들은 아이들이었지, 고양이가 아니었습니다. "그래서 뭐?"

"그러니까." 회색 수고양이가 말했습니다. "내가 바로 돌아가신 너의 훌륭한 줄리어스 증조할아버지(Great-Grandfather Julius)란 말이야."

2장

제가 막 귀엽고 작은 흑백의 새끼 고양이와 집에 가려는 참에, 갑자기 커다란 회색 수고양이가 자신이 저의 돌아가신 증조할아버지라고 말하고 있어요. 저는 무엇을 해야 할지 몰랐습니다. 저는 새끼 고양이를 다시 한 번 살펴봤습니다. 그는 사랑스럽게 자기 앞발을 핥고 있었습니다. 수고양이는 제가 여전히 새끼 고양이에게 마음이 기울어져 있는 것을 알았습니다.

"뭐야? 넌 내가 귀엽다고 생각하지 않아?" 그가 물었습니다. 그러더니 그는 귀여운 자세라고 자기가 생각한 게 분명한 자세를 취했습니다.

"할아버지는. . . 어느 정도는 귀여워요, 할아버지." 제가 말했습니다. "그건 그냥. . ."

"귀엽기는. 뭐가 귀엽다고 그래." 그가 말했습니다. "너 설마 나에게 화장실 교육도 제대로 받은 적 없고 벼룩이 들끓는 모르는 사람은 데리고 나가면서 너의 사랑하는 증조할아버지를 냄새나는 작은 우리 안에서 처박혀 지내도록 내버려 둘 거라고 말하려는 건 아니겠지? 가족은 가족이다, 잭."

저는 수고양이를, 그런 다음 새끼 고양이를, 그런 다음 수고양이를 바라봤습니다. *가족은 가족이다.* 재미있게도, 그것은 레아 할머니가 항상 하시는 말이었어요. 바로 그것 때문이었습니다.

"할아버지가 옳으신 것 같네요, 할아버지." 제가 말했습니다. "가족은 가족인 거죠."

"이제야 네가 맞는 말을 하는구나, 얘야." 고양이가 말했습니다. "그리고, 부탁이니, 나를 줄리어스 증조할아버지라고 부르렴."

3장

헉헉거리면서, 판지로 된 제 고양이 이동장을 들고, 제가 집에 도착했을 때, 아빠는 현관에서 저를 맞이했습니다.

제 부모님은 이혼했기 때문에, 저는 한동안은 아빠와 같이 지내고 한동안은 엄마와 같이 지냅니다.

"자." 웃으며, 그가 말했습니다. "네가 드디어 새끼 고양이를 갖게 된 것 같구나."

"네." 저는 말했고, 고양이 이동장을 내려놓았습니다. 저는 진이 다 빠져 있었습니다. 안에 있는 줄리어스 증조할아버지까지 포함해서, 그것은 분명 무게가 30파운드(약 13.6킬로그램) 가까이 나갔을 것입니다.

"내가 그 작은 친구를 봐도 될까?" 아빠가 물었습니다.

"그럼요, 아빠." 제가 말했습니다. "하지만 먼저 제가 아빠에게 두 가지 상황에 대해 말해야만 해요."

"그래, 뭔데?"

"음, 첫째로, 저는 새끼 고양이를 데려오지 않았어요. 저는 조금 나이 든 고양이를 데려왔어요."

"이런, 잭." 아빠가 말했습니다. "그건 정말 멋진 일이구나, 나이 든 고양이에게 집을 주다니. 나는 네가 아주 자랑스럽다, 얘야."

"으–흠. 그리고 둘째로, 그는 평범한 고양이가 아니에요, 아빠. 그는. . . 음, 우선, 그는 말을 해요."

"그가 말을 한다고." 아빠가 말했습니다.

"네, 그는 말을 해요."

제 농담에 맞춰 주기로 하고, 아빠는 미소를 지었습니다.

"알겠다. 그래, 그가 뭐라고 말하니?"

"그는 자기가 줄리어스 증조할아버지래요."

"나는 줄리어스 증조할아버지가 있었다는 것을 네가 기억할 거라고 생각조차 못 했구나." 싱긋 웃으며, 아빠가 말했습니다.

제가 기억하는 것은 정말 자상해서 거의 성자와 다름없었던, 그녀의 아버지, 줄리어스 증조할아버지에 대해서 레아 할머니가 계속 말하는 것을 들었던 일입니다. 그리고 나서 그녀는 언제나 줄리어스 증조할아버지가 그녀 남편의 아버지, 모리스 증조할아버지(Great-Grandfather Maurice)와 얼마나 정반대였는지 덧붙이곤 했습니다. 모리스 증조할아버지는 가족의 말썽꾼이었습니다.

지금까지, 줄리어스 증조할아버지는 저에게 그다지 성자같이 보이지 않았습니다. 저는 고양이 이동장을 열었습니다. 줄리어스 증조할아버지와 아빠는 꽤 오랫동안 서로를 자세히 살펴봤습니다.

"음, 그는 확실히. . . 크구나." 아빠가 말했습니다. "안녕하세요, 줄리어스 증조할아버지. 저를 기억하세요? 댄(Dan)

이요? 할아버지는 항상 제일 좋아하는 손주가 저라고 말하곤 하셨죠. 인사할 수 있으세요?"

줄리어스 증조할아버지는 뭔가를 말하려는 것처럼 보였습니다. 그러더니 대신에 그는 자기 뒷다리로 자신의 귀 뒤를 긁었습니다.

"그가 그다지 말하기를 좋아하지는 않는구나." 아빠가 말했습니다.

"아빠가 동물 보호소에서 그가 말하는 것을 들었어야 했어요." 제가 말했습니다.

고개를 가로저으며, 아빠는 싱긋 웃었고 걸어가 버렸습니다.

"어째서 아빠에게 말하지 않았어요?" 제가 물었습니다.

"나는 내가 원할 때 말해." 고양이가 말했습니다. "다른 사람들이 내가 말하기를 원할 때가 아니라. 있지, 잭, 너 뭔가 먹을 것 좀 있니? 나는 너무 배고파서 쥐라도 잡아먹을 수 있을 것 같구나."

저는 동물 보호소에서 사람들이 저에게 준 공짜 고양이 사료 캔을 가지고 있었습니다. 저는 그것을 바닥 위에 있는 그릇에 덜었습니다. 줄리어스 증조할아버지는 그것의 냄새를 맡았고 그의 코를 찡그렸습니다.

"웩!" 그가 말했습니다. "저게 도대체 *뭐냐*?"

"그레이비(gravy)에 넣은 소고기 부

산물이에요." 제가 대답했습니다.

"너 혹시 사워크림(sour cream)을 곁들인 청어를 좀 가지고 있니?"

저는 우리에게 그런 것이 없다고 그에게 말했습니다. 그는 이 말을 잘 받아들이지 않았습니다.

"이렇게 말해 줄게, 얘야." 줄리어스 증조할아버지가 말했습니다. "네가 당장 나에게 사워크림을 곁들인 청어를 가져오든가, 아니면 내가 네 소파에 오줌을 싸든가."

"그거 진심은 아니시겠죠." 제가 말했습니다.

"한 번 시험해 봐라." 그가 말했습니다.

개인적으로, 줄리어스 증조할아버지는 제가 들었던 것보다 훨씬 더 괴팍했습니다. 하지만 저는 이해하려고 노력했습니다. 죽었다가 고양이로 환생하는 것이 사람의 기분을 망칠 수 있다고 저는 생각했습니다.

4장

다행히도, 모퉁이에 있는 식료품점에서 사워크림을 곁들인 청어를 팔았습니다. 저는 그것을 줄리어스 증조할아버지에게 가져왔습니다.

"바로 그거야." 그가 그것을 보았을 때 그는 말했습니다. 그는 그것을 게걸스럽게 먹어 치웠습니다. "나쁘지 않군. 전혀 나쁘지 않아. 하지만 내일은, 잭, 식료품점 직원이 사워크림을 아끼지 않도록 확실히 해라."

맙소사, 이 고양이는 막무가내였습니다!

"들어 보세요, 제가 할아버지에게 청어와 사워크림을 매일 사 드릴 수는 없어요." 제가 말했습니다. "저는 일주일에 겨우 3달러를 용돈으로 받아요. 그리고 추수감사절 주말 동안은 제가 할아버지를 위해 그것을 살 수 없어요—저는 여기에 있지도 않을 거예요. 저는 시카고에 가요. 레아 할머니를 뵙기 위해서요."

"우리가 레아를 만나러 간다고?" 그가 기뻐하며 물었습니다.

"저는 그럴 거예요." 제가 말했습니다. "할아버지는 이웃 사람과 함께 여기에 있을 거예요."

"네가 시카고에 가는데 너는 내 딸을 만날 수 있게 나를 데려가 주지 않을 거라고? 내가 환생했는데 그녀를 보러 오지 않았다는 것을 레아가 듣게 된다면, 그녀는 좌절할 거야."

"음." 제가 말했습니다. "제가 아빠에게 물어볼게요."

"잭." 아빠가 말했습니다. "나는 기꺼이

농담에 맞춰 주고 싶단다. 하지만 우리 둘 다 고양이가 말할 수 없다는 것을 알잖니. 단지 네가 할머니에게 저 고양이가 그녀의 아버지라고 말할 때 레아 할머니의 표정을 보고 싶어서, 내가 그를 시카고에 데려가고 싶어진다는 것은 인정해야겠지만 말이야."

"아빠, 저는 정말로 그를 시카고에 데려가고 싶어요. 저는 그것이 그에게 아주 큰 의미가 있을 거라고 생각해요."

"좋은 생각이 있다." 아빠가 말했습니다. "네가 만약 그가 나에게 말하도록 할 수 있다면, 너는 그를 시카고에 데려갈 수 있어."

저는 제 방으로 돌아왔고, 거기에서 줄리어스 증조할아버지는 저의 야구 카드 수집품을 뒤지고 있었습니다.

"너는 그중에 루 게릭(Lou Gehrig), 타이 코브(Ty Cobb), 아니면 로저스 혼즈비(Rogers Hornsby) 카드가 있니?" 그가 물었습니다.

"아니요, 유감스럽게도 없어요."

"게릭과 혼즈비는 친절한 사람들이었지. 코브는 그렇게까지 친절하지는 않았고."

"제가 듣기로도 그랬대요."

"하지만 세 사람 모두 내 야구공에 사인해 줬지."

"할아버지가 실제로 루 게릭, 타이 코브, 그리고 로저스 혼즈비를 만났다는 말씀이세요?" 제가 말했습니다. 수고양이가 고개를 끄덕였습니다. "그들이 사인한 공은 어떻게 됐어요?"

"내가 가지고 있지."

"어디에 말이에요?"

"안전한 곳에, 그건 걱정하지 말아라. 그래서 네 아버지가 내가 시카고에 가도 된다고 했니?"

"한 가지 조건이 있다고 말했어요."

"그게 뭔데?"

"할아버지가 아빠에게 말을 해야만 해요. 아빠는 할아버지가 말할 수 있다는 것을 믿지 않는 것 같아요."

"그게 내가 해야 할 전부인 거야, 그에게 말하는 것?"

"그게 전부예요."

"좋아, 해 보자."

저는 거실로 조용히 들어가는, 줄리어스 증조할아버지를 따라갔고, 그곳에서 아빠는 신문을 읽고 있었습니다.

"아빠." 제가 말했습니다. "줄리어스 증조할아버지가 아빠에게 말할 것이 있대요."

"정말?" 아빠가 말했습니다. 그는 얼굴에 커다란 미소를 지으며, 그의 신문을 내려놓았고 고양이를 향해 몸을 돌렸습니다. "좋아요." 그가 말했습니다. "말해 주세요. 사람에서 고양이로 변할 때 가장 곤란한 부분이 무엇이었나요?"

줄리어스 증조할아버지는 잠시 말없

이 아빠를 쳐다봤습니다. 그런 다음 그는 그의 고개를 높이 들었고, 그의 입을 열었고, 말했습니다. "나에게는, 고양이 화장실에는 내 뒤로 잠글 수 있는 문이 없다는 사실을 알게 된 것이 가장 곤란한 부분이었던 것 같구나. 이 정도면 시카고로 여행을 가기에 충분하겠니?"

아빠의 두 눈이 머리 밖으로 곧장 불쑥 튀어나올 것처럼 휘둥그레졌습니다.

"저에게는 괜찮게 들리는데요." 제가 말했습니다. "어떠세요, 아빠?"

5장

아빠가 제 고양이가 줄리어스 증조할아버지라는 것을 알게 되자, 아빠는 그에게 죽는 것은 어떤지에 대해 계속 질문했습니다. 아빠는 우리가 시카고로 떠나기 전 이틀 동안, 그리고 공항으로 차를 타고 가는 긴 여정에서도 내내 멈추지 않았습니다.

"죽었다가 다시 살아난 사람들은 그들이 반대편 끝에 굉장히 밝은 빛이 있는 아주 긴 터널처럼 보이는 것을 지나왔다고 주장하죠." 아빠가 말했습니다. "그리고 그들의 죽은 친척들이 모두 반대편에서 그들을 맞이해 주었다고 했어요. 할아버지에게도 그런 일이 벌어졌나요?"

"나도 확실히 긴 터널을 지나서 반대편의 밝은 빛으로 나왔던 것을 기억해." 고양이를 운반하는 상자 안에서 줄리어스 증조할아버지가 말했습니다.

"그래요?" 아빠는 신나서 말했습니다.

"그럼." 줄리어스 증조할아버지가 말했습니다. "아마 그건 미드타운 터널(Midtown Tunnel)이었을 거야. 그리고 반대편의 밝은 빛은 퀸스(Queens)였고. 바로 그곳에 사람들이 나를 묻었거든. 있잖아. 혹시 시가(cigar)를 가지고 있니? 정말 좋은 시가를 피운 지가 몇 년이나 됐구나."

"할아버지는 시가를 피우는 것을 그만두셔야 해요." 제가 말했습니다. "그것들은 몸에 안 좋아요."

"네 말이 맞는 것 같구나." 줄리어스 증조할아버지가 말했습니다. "하지만 심지어 네가 죽고 나서도, 간절하게 원하는 것을 멈추지 못하는 것들이 있지."

"고양이로 지낸 지 얼마나 오래됐어요?" 아빠가 물어보았습니다.

"내가 운전 면허증을 안 가지고 있어서 말이다." 줄리어스 증조할아버지가 말했습니다. "내가 몇 살로 보이니?"

"열두 살에서 열세 살이요." 제가 말했습니다.

"대략 그쯤인 것 같구나." 그가 말했습니다. "물론, 내가 곧바로 고양이로 되살아난 건 아니었단다."

"아니었어요?"

"오 아니지. 처음에 나는 애벌레였어."

"애벌레요?" 제가 말했습니다. "그건 어땠어요?"

"엄청나게 지루했지. 나뭇잎을 먹는 게 거의 전부였어. 나는 나뭇잎을 먹으면서 그것들이 사워크림을 곁들인 청어라고 상상하려고 노력했단다. 자, 너 혹시라도 슈냅스(schnapps) 좀 가진 것 없니?"

"슈냅스가 뭐예요?" 제가 물었습니다.

"독한 술이야." 아빠가 말했습니다. "아니요, 죄송해요, 저에게는 슈냅스가 없어요."

우리는 공항에 도착했습니다. 아빠는 택시 기사에게 돈을 냈습니다. 저는 줄리어스 증조할아버지를 다시 고양이 이동장에 넣으려고 했습니다.

"이봐, 왜 이래." 그가 외쳤습니다. "나를 다시 여행 가방 속에서 여행하게 하지마. 나는 품위 있는 노인이라고, 제발."

"지난 생에서 할아버지는 품위 있는 노인이셨죠." 제가 말했습니다. "이번 생에서 할아버지는 길고양이예요. 그리고 고양이는 고양이 이동장 안에 들어가서 여행하죠."

줄리어스 증조할아버지는 한숨을 쉬었고 그의 이동장 안으로 들어갔습니다.

우리가 비행기에 타자, 아빠는 다시 질문을 시작했습니다.

"그래서, 줄리어스 할아버지." 아빠가 말했습니다. "애벌레가 된 후에는, 나비가 됐나요?"

"아니, 나방이었어." 고양이 이동장 안에서 목소리가 말했습니다. "대부분 스웨터를 먹는 게 전부였지."

"스웨터를 먹었다고요?" 제가 말했습니다. "웩!"

"직접 해 보기 전에는 함부로 말하지마라." 줄리어스 증조할아버지가 말했습니다. "어느 질 좋은 캐시미어 터틀넥 스웨터(cashmere turtleneck)가 기억나는구나. 거의 호밀빵 위에 얹은 콘드 비프(corned beef)만큼이나 맛있었단다. 그러던 어느 날 밤에 나는 폴리네시아(Polynesian) 식당 밖에 있던 횃불에 지나치게 가까이 가게 됐고—푸슈우!"

"또 다른 터널이요?"

"아니, 아니, 나방은 터널을 지나가지 않아. 사람만 터널을 지난단다. 그 후에 나는 쥐가 됐어."

"그리고 치즈를 먹는 게 전부였겠네요, 제 생각엔." 아빠가 말했습니다.

"아니, 목재를 먹는 게 전부였어. 묻지도 마라."

"잠깐만요." 제가 말했습니다. "처음에 할아버지는 애벌레였다가, 그다음 나방이었다가, 그다음 쥐가 되었잖아요. 어떻게 이 모든 것들이 될 시간이 있었어요?"

"우리는 지금 많은 시간을 이야기하는 게 아니란다." 줄리어스 증조할아버지가 말했습니다. "너는 죽었다가, 애벌레로 살고, 그다음 나방으로, 그다음 쥐가 되었는데도, 목요일로부터 일주일이 지난 후에 다시 돌아올 수도 있어. 하지만 시간은 나에게 중요하지 않았지. 나는 죽었거든. 나에게는 꽤 많은 여가 시간이 주어졌단다."

"실례합니다." 승무원이 우리 줄을 지나가며 그녀는 말했습니다. "이륙 준비를 위해, 안전벨트가 단단히 채워져 있는지 그리고 여러분의 좌석 등받이와 접이식 테이블이 똑바로 놓여 있고 고정되어 있는지 확인해 주시기 바랍니다."

"이봐, 아가씨." 줄리어스 증조할아버지가 말했습니다. "비행 후에 무엇을 할 예정이야?"

승무원은 아빠가 그 말을 했다고 생각했기 때문에, 아빠를 째려봤습니다.

그리고 우리는 안전벨트를 맸습니다. 다음은—시카고입니다!

6장

"우리가 그녀를 만나기 전에, 나는 너에게 한 가지 물어보고 싶구나." 레아 할머니가 사시는 레이크 쇼어 드라이브(Lake Shore Drive)에 있는 건물 엘리베이터에서 아빠가 말했습니다.

"무엇을요?" 제가 물었습니다.

"레아 할머니는 80대란다. 너는 정말로 80대 여성에게 그녀의 돌아가신 아버지가 지금은 고양이라고 말하는 것이 안전하다고 생각하니?"

"레아 할머니는 아주 기운이 넘치시고, 편견이 없는 사람이잖아요." 제가 대답했습니다. "저는 할머니가 그 소식을 잘 받아들이실 거라고 확신해요."

7층에서 엘리베이터 문이 열렸고 아빠가 우리의 짐을 들고 저는 줄리어스 증조할아버지가 안에 들어 있는 이동장을 든 채, 우리는 레아 할머니의 아파트를 향해 복도를 따라 걸어갔습니다.

레아 할머니는 우리를 보고 매우 기뻐했습니다. 그녀는 계속해서 우리를 끌어안고 여기저기 입을 맞추었습니다. 우리가 모두 그녀의 아파트에 편하게 앉았을 때 처음으로 그녀는 고양이 이동장을 알아챘습니다.

"설마 동물을 데리고 시카고까지 이 먼 길을 온 건 아니겠지?" 그녀가 말했습니다.

"그냥 아무 동물이 아니에요, 할머니." 제가 말했습니다. "아주 특별한 동물이에요."

"어떤 점에서 특별하니?" 레아 할머니가 물었습니다.

"그가 고양이일 뿐만 아니라, 또 우리

가족의 일원이라는 점에서 특별해요." 제가 말했습니다.

"다시 말하면, 네가 그를 너무 사랑해서 너는 마치 그가 우리 가족의 일원인 것처럼 느낀다는 거니?" 레아 할머니가 물었습니다.

저는 아빠를 쳐다본 뒤 다시 레아 할머니를 쳐다봤습니다.

"아뇨." 제가 말했습니다. "그가 정말로 우리 가족의 일원이라는 뜻이에요."

그리고 그 말과 함께 저는 고양이 이동장을 열었습니다. 레아 할머니와 줄리어스 증조할아버지가 처음으로 서로를 바라봤습니다.

"레아 할머니." 제가 말했습니다. "저는 이 고양이가 할머니의 아버지, 줄리어스 증조할아버지라고 생각해요."

레아 할머니는 잠시 조용히 고양이를 쳐다보았고 그러고 나서 그녀의 고개를 가로저었습니다.

"아니야." 그녀가 말했습니다. "나는 그렇게 생각하지 않아. 내 아버지는 좀 더 키가 크셨어."

"사랑스러운 레아." 줄리어스 증조할아버지가 말했습니다. "너를 다시 보니 정말 좋구나. 이 모든 세월 동안 어떻게 지냈니, 우리 딸?"

"그것이 나한테 말을 하고 있어." 레아 할머니가 아주 이상한 목소리로 말했습니다. "고양이가 나에게 영어로 말을 하고 있어."

"맞아요." 제가 말했습니다.

"사랑스러운 레아야." 줄리어스 증조할아버지가 말했습니다. "내가 고양이인 것은 맞지만, 나는 네 아버지이기도 해."

"그것이 아직도 나한테 말을 하고 있어." 레아 할머니가 말했습니다. "내가 맞지, 고양이가 아직도 나에게 말하고 있는 거지?"

"할머니가 맞아요." 제가 말했습니다.

"내가 그것은 내 아버지가 아니라고 했다고 고양이에게 전하렴." 그녀가 말했습니다.

"그에게 직접 말하지 그러세요?" 제가 권했습니다.

"나는 고양이하고는 말하지 않아." 레아 할머니가 똑같이 이상한 목소리로 말했습니다.

"레아 할머니가 말하기를 할아버지는 할머니의 아버지가 아니래요." 제가 말했습니다.

"나도 그녀의 말을 들었다, 나도 들었다고." 줄리어스 증조할아버지가 말했습니다. "내가 뭐, 귀가 안 들리니?" 그런 다음 고양이는 그의 목소리를 누그러뜨렸습니다. "사랑스러운 레아야, 나를 기억하지 못하겠니? 아빠(Daddy)란다!"

"내가 우리는 절대 아버지를 아빠라

는 이름으로 부르지 않았다고 했다고 고양이에게 전하렴." 레아 할머니가 말했습니다. "그것에게 우리가 내 진짜 아버지를 뭐라고 불렀는지 물어봐."

"자신이 할아버지를 무슨 이름으로 불렀는지 할머니가 물어보시네요?" 제가 물었습니다.

"나도 그녀의 말을 들었다, 나도 들었어." 줄리어스 증조할아버지의 목소리가 높아지고 있었습니다. "너는 그녀가 하는 모든 말을 반복하지 않아도 돼."

"자 그렇다면, 할머니가 할아버지를 무슨 이름으로 불렀어요?"

"그건 아빠가 아니었지." 줄리어스 증조할아버지가 말했습니다.

"우리는 이미 아빠가 아니었다고 어머니가 말하는 것을 들었어요." 아빠가 말했습니다.

"물론 그건 아빠가 아니었지." 줄리어스 증조할아버지가 말했습니다. "왜냐하면 그건. . . 아버지(Father)였기 때문이야."

ˊ레아 할머니가 고개를 가로저었습니다.

"고양이에게 그건 아버지가 아니었다고 말하렴." 레아 할머니가 말했습니다.

"할머니가 말씀하시길 그건—"

"반복하지 말아라!" 줄리어스 증조할아버지가 화가 나서 날카롭게 말했습니다. 그런 다음 그는 빠르게 자신의 침착함을 회복했습니다. "그건 아버지가 아니었지. 물론 그건 아버지가 아니었어." 그가 말했습니다. "아버지는 내가 나 자신을 불렀던 말이지. 네가 나를 불렀던 호칭은. . . 파파(Papa)였어."

"고양이에게 그건 파파가 아니었다고 말하렴." 레아 할머니가 말했습니다.

"오 맙소사." 줄리어스 증조할아버지가 말했습니다. "내가 지금 당장 좋은 시가 한 대를 피거나 슈냅스 한 잔을 즐길 수 있었더라면. 사랑스러운 레아야, 나는 백 살이 넘었단다. 나는 애벌레였다가, 나방이었다가, 생쥐로 살았어. 나는 여러 번 죽었고, 그래서 내 기억은 예전같지 않단다. 제발 이번엔 너그럽게 봐주고 네가 나를 뭐라고 부르곤 했는지 나에게 말해 주겠니?"

"어서요, 레아 할머니." 제가 말했습니다. "할머니가 그를 뭐라고 부르고는 했는지 그에게 말해 주세요."

"나는 고양이를 아무 이름으로도 부르지 않았어." 그녀가 말했습니다. "나는 나의 아버지—내 진짜 아버지, 내 인간 아버지를—파피(Pappy)라고 불렀지."

"파피나, 그거나." 줄리어스 증조할아버지가 말했습니다. 그는 무시하듯이 그의 발을 흔들었습니다. "파피가 파파하고 얼마나 다르다고 그래?"

"잠깐만." 레아 할머니가 말했습니다.

"내가 방금 뭔가를 깨달았어."

"그게 뭔데요?" 제가 말했습니다.

"고양이가 좋은 시가 한 대나 슈냅스 한 잔을 원한다고 말했니?"

"그렇게 말했죠." 제가 말했습니다.

"나의 아버지, 줄리어스는, 시가를 절대로 피우지 않았어. 그리고 그는 슈냅스도 전혀 마시지 않았지. 누가 시가를 피우고 슈냅스를 마셨는지 아니?"

"누구인데요?" 제가 말했습니다.

"누구인가요?" 아빠가 말했습니다.

"가족의 말썽꾼, 바로 그 사람이야. 네 고양이는 거짓말쟁이야, 잭. 그는 내 아버지, 줄리어스가 아니야, 절대로. 그는 네 할아버지의 쓸모없는 아버지란다. 그는 모리스 증조할아버지야!"

7장

"레아 할머니가 말하신 것이 사실이에요?" 저는 커다란 회색 수고양이에게 따졌습니다. "할아버지가 제 할아버지의 쓸모없는 아버지, 모리스인가요?"

"자, 침착해라, 얘야, 침착해라." 그가 말했습니다. "일단, 그녀가 어떻게 감히 나를 쓸모없는 사람이라고 부를 수가 있어?"

"어떻게 내가 감히 그럴 수 있냐고요?" 레아 할머니가 화를 내며 말했습니다. "제가 어떻게 감히 그러는지 말해 줄게요. 당신은 당신의 정신 나간 발명품을 만들기 위해 제 아버지의 돈 가운데 3만 달러를 가져갔어요. 그리고 나서 당신은 마을을 떠났죠. 사라졌어요. 우리는 다시는 당신으로부터 한마디도 듣지 못했어요."

우리는 모두 고양이 쪽으로 몸을 돌렸습니다.

"무슨 발명품이요?" 제가 물었습니다.

"내가 너에게 어떤 발명품이었는지 말해 줄게." 레아 할머니가 말했습니다. "대머리수리를 위한 부분 가발이 그 중 하나였지."

"누가 대머리수리를 위해 부분 가발을 사겠어요?" 저는 고양이에게 물었습니다.

"뭐, 그게 문제였지." 고양이가 말했습니다.

"그다음엔 개를 부르는 호각이 있었어." 레아 할머니가 말을 계속 이었습니다. "단지 개들만이 그것을 들을 수 있었어야 했지."

"그건 좀 낫네요." 제가 말했습니다.

"한 가지 사소한 점만 제외한다면 말이야." 그녀가 말했습니다. 고양이는 당황하는 것처럼 보였습니다. "개들도 그것을 듣지 못했단다. 그것을 불면 동네의 모든 쥐들이 뛰쳐나왔지."

"잘 작동하는 것을 발명하기는 했어
요?" 제가 물었습니다.

"했지!" 고양이가 말했습니다. "핫도
그 빵(hot dog bun) 모양의 닥스훈트
(dachshund)용 스웨터야. 아주 귀여워,
내 입으로 말하긴 좀 그렇지만. 처음에
는 그것이 팔리지 않았어. 나는 내가 줄
리어스의 돈을 모두 잃었다고 생각했지,
그래서 마을 밖으로 도망쳤어. 그런데
그거 아니? 얼마 뒤에 그 스웨터가 미친
듯이 팔리기 시작했단다. 닥스훈트를
가진 사람이라면 모두 그것을 가져야만
했지. 나는 3만 달러를 모두 되찾았지.
나는 그것을 곧장 시카고에 있는 비밀
은행 계좌로 보냈어."

"비밀 계좌요?" 제가 말했습니다.

"시카고 모턴 F. 아크로폴리스 상호
저축 은행(Morton F. Acropolis Savings
and Loan Association of Chicago)에
있단다." 고양이가 말했습니다. "내가
줄리어스에게 돈을 갚기 위해서 시카고
로 오고 있었을 때 나는 그레이하운드
버스(Greyhound bus)에 치였어."

우리는 모두 고양이를 빤히 쳐다봤습
니다.

"모리스 증조할아버지." 제가 부드럽
게 말했습니다. "할아버지는 우리에게
사실이 아닌 많은 것을 말했어요. 할아
버지가 우리에게 지금 말하고 있는 것
이 사실인지 우리가 어떻게 알죠?"

"내일 아침에 제일 먼저." 그가 말했
습니다. "나를 시카고 모턴 F. 아크로폴
리스 상호 저축 은행으로 데려가. 그러
면 너희는 알게 될 거야."

8장

그래서 다음 날 아침, 아침 식사 직후
에, 아빠, 레아 할머니, 모리스 증조할
아버지, 그리고 저는 모두 택시를 타고
시카고 모턴 F. 아크로폴리스 상호 저축
은행으로 갔습니다.

우리가 이야기를 나눈 은행 직원은
처음에 모리스가 우리에게 줬던 번호를
가진 비밀 계좌를 전혀 찾을 수 없다고
말했습니다.

"그녀에게 더 열심히 찾아보라고 말
해라." 모리스가 고양이 이동장 안에서
말했습니다.

은행 직원은 놀란 듯이 보였습니다.

"좀 더 열심히 찾아봐 주세요." 제가
말했습니다.

그래서 은행 직원은 더 열심히 찾았
습니다.

"이것에 대해서 우리에게 사실을 말
하는 편이 좋을 거예요." 제가 고양이
이동장에 대고 말했습니다.

"그렇게 의심하지 마." 고양이 이동장
안에서 목소리가 말했습니다.

은행 직원이 돌아왔습니다.

"제가 뭔가를 찾기는 찾았어요." 그녀가 말했습니다. "아주 오래전에 계좌 하나가 열렸어요. 저는 이게 맞는 것인지 모르겠네요. 하지만 이것은 여러분이 저에게 준 것과 같은 번호로 되어 있기는 해요."

"계좌에 적힌 이름이 뭐예요?" 제가 물었습니다.

"그건, 물론, 비밀이에요." 은행 직원이 말했습니다.

"만약 제가 당신에게 이름을 말한다면요?" 제가 말했습니다. "만약에 제가 맞으면 그냥 고개를 끄덕여 줄 수 있나요?"

"당신은 무슨 이름을 생각하고 있나요?" 그녀가 물었습니다.

"모리스요." 제가 말했습니다.

은행 직원이 고개를 끄덕였습니다.

"제가 맞군요!" 제가 말했습니다. 모리스 증조할아버지가 사실을 말하고 있었습니다! "이제 저희가 그 돈을 어떻게 찾을 수 있나요?"

"음, 계좌에 이름이 적힌 사람이 그렇게 하겠다고 서명해야 한단다." 그녀가 말했습니다.

우리는 모두 서로를 쳐다봤습니다.

"만약에 그가 그것을 할 수 없다면요?" 제 아빠가 물었습니다.

"왜 그가 그것을 할 수 없나요?" 은행 직원이 말했습니다.

"만약에 그가. . . 그에게 만약에 어떤 일이 일어났다면요?" 제가 말했습니다.

"예를 들면 무슨 일?" 은행 직원이 말했습니다.

"예를 들면, 어, 글쎄요, 예를 들면 그가 고양이로 변했다거나." 제가 말했습니다.

"예를 들면 그가 죽었다거나." 아빠가 재빨리 말했습니다.

"음, 만약 계좌 소유자가 사망했다면." 은행 직원이 말했습니다. "그러면 그 돈은 공증에 들어가요. 공증은 아주 길고, 아주 복잡한 법적 절차예요. 처리하는 데 몇 년이 걸리죠."

"사망이 무슨 뜻이에요?" 제가 소곤거렸습니다.

"죽었다는 거야." 고양이 이동장 안에서 목소리가 말했습니다.

"만약에 그가 고양이로 변했다면요?" 제가 물었습니다.

"뭐라고요?" 은행 직원이 말했습니다.

저의 아빠는 저를 보았고 그의 고개를 가로저었습니다.

"당신은 환생을 믿으세요?" 저는 은행 직원에게 물었습니다.

"아니요." 그녀가 말했습니다.

우리는 모두 서로를 쳐다봤습니다. 우리는 다음에 어떻게 해야 할지 아무 생각도 못했습니다.

"얘." 고양이 이동장 안에서 목소리가 말했습니다. "내가 그녀에게 말해도 되겠니?"

"그 동물 이동장 안에 누가 있나요?" 불안해하며, 은행 직원이 물었습니다.

"이봐, 나를 여기서 나가게 해 줘!" 목소리가 말했습니다.

저는 제 아빠를 쳐다봤습니다. 그는 어깨를 으쓱 올렸습니다. 저는 고양이 이동장을 열었습니다. 모리스 증조할아버지가 카운터 위로 뛰어나왔습니다.

"어, 유감스럽게도 애완동물은 은행 안에 있을 수 없어요." 은행 직원이 말했습니다. "규정에서 분명히 금지하고—"

"오, 잠깐 조용히 해 봐, 아가씨." 모리스 증조할아버지가 말했습니다. "그리고 어쩌면 우리는 이걸 해결할 수 있을 거야."

은행 직원은 기절할 것처럼 보였습니다.

"이쪽은요." 제가 말했습니다. "제 증조할아버지, 모리스예요. 그가 아직 사람이었던 오래전에 그는 당신의 은행에서 계좌를 만들었어요."

은행 직원은 자신이 쓰러지지 않도록 카운터에 크게 기댔습니다.

"이 사람은, 정말로, 그렇게 보이네요 . . . 고양이인 것처럼." 그녀가 소곤거렸습니다.

습니다.

"두말하면 잔소리지." 모리스 증조할아버지가 말했습니다. "그리고 괜찮다면, 나는 내 계좌에 있는 모든 돈을 찾아서 내 가족에게 주고 싶어."

"당신이 그렇게 하겠다고 서명을. . . 할 수 있나요?" 간신히 말을 할 수 있어서, 그녀가 소곤거렸습니다.

"이봐, 귀여운 아가씨." 그가 말했습니다. "나는 고양이야. 알아차렸겠지만. 나는 마주 보는 엄지손가락조차도 없다고. 그러니까 나는 펜을 잡을 수가 없어."

"당신이 서명할 수 없다면." 그녀가 속삭였습니다. "우리는 당신에게 돈을 드릴 수가. . . 없어요."

"도대체 왜 안 돼?" 그가 물었습니다.

"그건. . . 회사 정책과 맞지 않아요." 이제는 눈을 질끈 감은 채로, 그녀가 소곤거렸습니다.

"그러면 회사 정책을 바꾸는 건 어떤가?" 그가 말했습니다. "이제부터는, 누군가 고양이로 환생해서 그의 돈을 찾으러 올 때는 언제든지, 그가 그저 그렇게 해 달라고 요청하기만 하면 된다고. 어때?"

은행 직원은 크게 심호흡을 했습니다.

"저는 그저. . . 우리가 그렇게 할 수 있는지 모르겠어요." 그녀가 말했습니다.

"좋아 그러면, 모티(Morty)를 불러 주게." 모리스 증조할아버지가 말했습니다.

"모티가 누구죠?" 은행 직원이 물었습니다.

"모티가 누구죠?" 모리스 증조할아버지가 따라서 말했습니다. "당신 지금 이 은행의 창립자, 모턴 F. 아크로폴리스를 모른다는 말이야?"

그리고 그 말과 함께, 고양이는 카운터에서 뛰어내려왔고 부리나케 복도를 따라 달려갔습니다.

"저 거기 잠시만요." 은행 직원이 그를 불렀습니다. "저는 당신을 그렇게 하도록 둘 수—"

모리스 증조할아버지는 화려한 문 앞에서 멈췄습니다. 앞에는 "모턴 F. 아크로폴리스"라고 쓰여 있었습니다.

"이봐, 모티!" 모리스 증조할아버지가 소리쳤습니다. "자네 거기 있나?"

"모리스?" 사무실 안에서 놀란 목소리가 외쳤습니다. "모리스, 자네인가?"

고양이는 그의 코로 창립자의 사무실 문을 밀어서 열었고 안으로 걸어 들어갔습니다. 아빠, 레아 할머니, 그리고 제가 바짝 뒤에 붙어서 따라갔습니다. 우리 바로 뒤를 따라 은행 직원이 왔습니다.

일종의 골동품처럼 보이는 기다란 책상 뒤에 제가 이제까지 본 사람 중에 가장 나이 든 사람이 앉아 있었습니다. 그는 가장 작은 사람 가운데 한 명이기도 했습니다. 저는 그가 저보다 훨씬 더 키가 클까 의심스러웠고, 그는 놀랍도록 두꺼운 렌즈가 들어간 안경을 쓰고 있었습니다.

"이봐, 모티, 만나서 반갑네!" 고양이가 말했습니다.

"모리스, 이 늙은 녀석 같으니, 자네인가?" 아크로폴리스 씨(Mr. Acropolis)가 소리쳤습니다. 그는 그의 안경을 통해 눈을 가늘게 뜨고 보면서 그의 책상 너머를 자세히 봤습니다. "내 눈이 예전에 그랬던 것 같지가 않아. 하지만 나는 저 목소리를 어디서라도 알아차릴 수 있지, 심지어 이렇게 오랜 세월이 흐른 후에도!"

"그래서 어떻게 지냈나, 모티?"

"나는 신경 쓰지 말게, 자네는 어떻게 지냈어, 모리스? 나는 자네가 죽었다고 들었어."

"그랬지." 고양이가 말했습니다. "하지만 나는 이제 괜찮아. 들어 보게, 모티, 나에게 문제가 생겼어. 아마 자네가 나를 도와줄 수 있을 것 같네."

"자네를 위해서 말인가, 모리스? 무엇이든지. 내가 무엇을 하면 되나?"

"회장님." 은행 직원이 말했습니다. "혹시 알고 계신가요 지금 회장님과 말하고 있는 것이 고—"

"조용히 해, 롤라(Lola)." 노인이 날카롭게 말했습니다. "나는 이 사람을 오랫동안 보지 못했어."

"하지만 그는 사람이 아니에요, 회장님." 은행 직원이 말했습니다. "그는 고—"

"조용히 해!" 아크로폴리스 씨가 소리쳤습니다. "계속하게, 모리스, 내가 자네를 위해 무엇을 도와주면 되겠나?"

"내가 핫도그 스웨터로 벌었던 돈 말이야, 모티. 나는 그것을 내 계좌에서 인출하고 싶다네. 하지만 여기 이 젊은 아가씨가 나에게 내가 그럴 수 없다고 말하더군."

"허튼소리!" 아크로폴리스 씨가 고함쳤습니다. "나는 직접 그 핫도그 스웨터에 투자했어. 내가 했던 것 중에 가장 영리한 행동이었지. 그 사람에게 그의 돈을 줘, 롤라!"

"하지만 아크로폴리스 씨, 그는 서명할 수가 없어요."

"왜 그런가?"

"그는 자신의 발(paw)로 펜을 쥘 수가 없어요." 그녀가 말했습니다.

"뭐, 나도 내 손(paw)으로 펜을 쥘 수가 없어." 아크로폴리스 씨가 말했습니다. "사람이 우리 나이가 되면, 애야, 더는 스스로 할 수 없는 일들이 있단다. 그를 도와주게, 제발!"

"아—알겠습니다, 회장님." 은행 직원이 말했습니다.

그렇게 우리는 모두 아크로폴리스 씨의 사무실에서 나왔습니다. 그런 다음, 떨리는 손으로, 은행 직원이 고양이의 발 사이에 펜을 끼웠고 그가 자신의 이름을 서명하도록 도와줬습니다. 그리고 그녀는 수표를 써서 그것을 우리에게 건넸습니다. 아빠는 액수를 보고 휘파람을 불었습니다.

"모리스 할아버지, 할아버지가 이 계좌에 3만 달러가 있다고 말했던 것 같은데요." 그가 말했습니다.

"거기에 얼마나 있나?" 모리스가 물었습니다.

"9만 달러 가까이요." 아빠가 말했습니다.

"9만 달러라고?" 레아 할머니가 물었습니다. 그것은 우리가 은행에 도착한 이후로 그녀가 처음 말한 것이었습니다.

"음, 30년보다 더 긴 세월에 대한 이자가 붙었으니까요." 아빠가 말했습니다.

"그리고 할아버지는 정말로 우리가 이것을 갖기를 바라나요?" 제가 물었습니다.

"한 가지 조건이 있어." 모리스 증조할아버지가 말했습니다.

"그게 뭔데요?"

"너희가 나에게 팜비치(Palm Beach)로 가는 일등석, 편도 티켓과, 매일 아침에는 청어와 사워크림, 그리고 매일 밤에는 슈냅스 한 잔을 정기적으로 받는 것까지 포함된, 고급 애완동물 호텔의 몇 년 치 임대료를, 나에게 충분할 만큼 남겨 주는 거지."

"우리와 같이 살지 않을 거예요?" 제가 말했습니다.

"내가 너를 사랑하는 만큼 말이다, 잭." 모리스 증조할아버지가 말했습니다. "나는 언제나 내 노년을 플로리다주(Florida)에서 보내고 싶었단다. 나는 다소 투기적인 성향을 지닌 발명품에 몇 달러쯤 기꺼이 투자할 사람들이 그곳에 있다는 것을 알거든."

그래서 모리스 증조할아버지는 플로리다주에서 풍족한 삶을 살기 위해 떠났습니다. 하지만 그가 그렇게 하기 전에 그는 은행 직원에게 그의 안전 금고를 열도록 했습니다. 거기에 그것이 있었습니다. 루 게릭, 타이 코브, 로저스 혼즈비가 사인한 야구공이 말이에요.

"네 것이란다, 얘야." 그가 저에게 말했습니다. "나는 이것을 간직하려고 했어, 하지만 봐, 도대체 나이 든 야옹이에게 오래된 야구공이 왜 필요하겠어?"

모리스 증조할아버지는 좀 막무가내이기는 했지만, 저는 그가 떠나는 것을 보게 되자 정말 슬펐습니다.

"이봐, 잭." 그가 말했습니다. "기운

내라. 이제 너는 동물 보호소로 돌아가서 네가 보고 있었던 그 작은 턱시도 새끼 고양이를 데려올 수 있어."

"하지만 할아버지가 말하기를 그는 벼룩과 기생충이 있고 고양이 화장실 쓰는 법도 결코 배우지 못했다고 했잖아요." 제가 대답했습니다.

"아마 그럴 테지." 그가 말했습니다. "하지만 그에게는 네가 그 모든 것을 눈감아 주게 할 만한 한 가지가 있단다."

"뭔데요?"

"전생에 그는 베이브 루스(Babe Ruth)였어."

Chapter 1

1. C I was in the animal shelter near our home in New York City. After years of begging my dad for a cat, he finally broke down and said yes. I could get a kitten. So here I was.

2. B "Sssst! Young man!" Someone was calling me. The voice sounded raspy and strange. "Hello, little boy! Over here!"

3. D "You can talk!" I said, hardly able to believe my ears. I moved closer to his cage. I wanted to see if his cat lips moved when he talked. Maybe this was just a trick—somebody doing ventriloquism. I mean I told you I like weird stuff, but this was really far out, even for me.

4. A "OK," the cat went on. "I didn't want to have to use this. But here goes: If you don't adopt me, they're going to put me to sleep. And I don't mean tuck me in bed in my jammies either. I mean kill me. You really want that on your conscience, kid?" "Listen, they don't put cats to sleep here," I said. "That is a well-known fact."

5. B "What's my name?" "Zack." "How—how did you know that?" I asked. I had to admit I was pretty impressed. Not that many people know my name, and even fewer cats. "You're impressed, huh?" said the big gray tomcat. "What if I told you I'm a member of your family, Zack?"

Chapter 2

1. D One minute I'm about to go home with a cute little black-and-white kitten, the next a big gray tomcat tells me he's my dead great-grandfather. I didn't know what to do.

2. A I took another look at the kitten. He was licking his front paw in an adorable way. The tomcat saw I was still leaning toward the kitten. "What? You don't think I'm cute?" he asked. Then he posed in what he must have thought was a cute pose.

3. C I took another look at the kitten. He was licking his front paw in an adorable way. The tomcat saw I was still leaning toward the kitten. "What? You don't think I'm cute?" he asked. Then he posed in what he must have thought was a cute pose. "You're . . . kind of cute, sir," I said.

4. A "You can't tell me you're going to walk out of here with a flea-bitten stranger who hasn't been properly toilet-trained and leave your beloved great-grandfather rotting in a stinking little cage? Family is family, Zack."

5. B Family is family. Funny, that's something Grandma Leah always says. That did it.

Chapter 3

1. A "And number two, he's not an ordinary cat, Dad. He's . . . well, for one thing, he talks." "He talks," said my dad. "Yeah, he talks." My dad smiled, deciding to go along with my little joke.

2. A What I remembered was hearing Grandma Leah go on about her father, Julius, who was so nice he was practically a saint. Then she'd always add how Julius was the complete opposite of Great-Grandpa Maurice, her husband's father. Maurice was the black sheep of the family.

3. B "Hello, Great-Grandpa Julius. Remember me? Dan? You always used to say I was your favorite grandchild. Can you say hello?"

4. D "How come you didn't talk to my dad?" I asked. "I talk when I want to," said the cat, "not when other people want me to."

5. C "You got maybe a little herring with sour cream?" I told him we didn't have anything like that. He did not take this at all well.

Chapter 4

1. B "Listen, I can't buy you herring and sour cream every day," I said. "I only get three dollars a week allowance. And I won't be able to buy it for you over Thanksgiving weekend—I won't even be here. I'm going to Chicago. To visit Grandma Leah."

2. D "You'd go to Chicago and you wouldn't take me to see my own daughter? If Leah heard I was reincarnated and didn't come to see her, she'd be crushed."

"Well," I said, "let me ask my dad."

3. C "I'll tell you what," said my dad. "If you can get him to talk to me, you can take him to Chicago."

4. C "You have any cards with Lou Gehrig, Ty Cobb, or Rogers Hornsby on them?" he asked. "No, I'm afraid not." "Gehrig and Hornsby were nice fellas. Cobb not so nice." "That's what I hear." "But all three signed my baseball." "You're saying you actually met Lou Gehrig, Ty Cobb, and Rogers Hornsby?" I said. The tomcat nodded. "What happened to the ball they signed?" "I have it." "Where?" "In a safe place, don't worry about it."

5. A "All right," he said. "Tell me. What was the hardest part about changing from a person into a cat?"

Chapter 5

1. A "Some people who died and were brought back to life again claim they went through what looked like a very long tunnel with very bright light at the other end," said my dad. "And all their dead relatives met them on the other side. Did that happen to you?"

2. B "How long have you been a cat?" asked my dad. "I don't have a driver's license on me," said Great-Grandpa Julius. "How old do I look?" "About twelve or thirteen," I said. "That feels about right," he said.

3. C "Oh no. First I was a caterpillar." "A caterpillar?" I said. "What was that like?" "Extremely boring. Mostly it was about eating leaves."

4. D Once we got on the plane, Dad started in again with his questions.

5. B "We're not talking about a lot of time here," said Great-Grandpa Julius. "You could die, do a stretch as a caterpillar, then a moth, then a mouse, and you could still be back by a week from Thursday."

Chapter 6

1. C "Grandma Leah," I said, "I believe this is your father, Great-Grandpa Julius." Grandma Leah stared at the cat in silence for a moment and then shook

her head. "No," she said. "I don't believe it is. My father was taller."

2. A "Tell the cat I said it's not my father," she said. "Why don't you tell him yourself?" I suggested. "I don't talk to cats," said Grandma Leah in the same strange voice.

3. D "She says what name did she call you?" I asked. "I heard her, I heard her." Great-Grandpa Julius's voice was rising. "You don't have to repeat everything she says."

4. B "Leah dear, I'm over a hundred years old. I've been a caterpillar, a moth, a mouse. I've died many times, so my memory isn't quite what it used to be."

5. C "Did the cat say it wanted a good cigar or a glass of schnapps?" "That's what he said," I said. "My father, Julius, never smoked cigars. And he never drank schnapps. You know who smoked cigars and drank schnapps?" "Who?" I said. "Who?" said my dad. "The black sheep of the family, that's who."

Chapter 7

1. D "I'll tell you where I get off. You took thirty thousand dollars of my father's money to work on your crazy inventions. Then you left town. Disappeared. We never heard a word from you again."

2. C We all turned to the cat. "What inventions?" I asked. "I'll tell you what inventions," said Grandma Leah. "A hairpiece for bald eagles was one." "Who would ever buy a hairpiece for bald eagles?" I asked the cat. "Well, that was a problem," said the cat. "Then there was the dog whistle," Grandma Leah went on. "Only dogs were supposed to be able to hear it."

3. D "A sweater for dachshunds in the shape of a hot dog bun. Very cute, if I do say so myself. At first it didn't sell. I thought I'd lost all of Julius's money, so I beat it out of town. But you know what? After a while that sweater started selling like crazy. Everybody who owned a dachshund had to have one. I made back the whole thirty thousand."

4. B "I made back the whole thirty thousand. I had it sent directly to a secret bank account in Chicago."

5. C "Great-Grandpa Maurice," I said gently. "You've told us many things that weren't true. How do we know what you're telling us now is the truth?"

Chapter 8

1. B "Now how do we get the money?" "Well, the individual whose name is on the account would have to sign for it," she said. We all looked at each other. "What if he couldn't do that?" asked my dad.

2. A "Who's Morty?" repeated Great-Grandpa Maurice. "You mean to say you don't know Morton F. Acropolis, the founder of the bank?"

3. C "Maurice, you old dog, is that you?" cried Mr. Acropolis. He squinted through his glasses and peered over the top of his desk. "My eyes aren't what they used to be. But I'd recognize that voice anywhere, even after all these years!"

4. D "But, Mr. Acropolis, he's unable to sign for it." "Why's that?" "He can't hold a pen in his paws," she said. "Well, I can't hold a pen in my paws either," said Mr. Acropolis. "A man gets to be our age, dear, there are certain things he can't do by himself any longer."

5. A "Ninety thousand dollars?" asked Grandma Leah. It was the first thing she'd said since we'd arrived at the bank. "Well, that's after more than thirty years of interest," said my dad. "And you really want us to have this?" I asked. "On one condition," said Maurice. "What's that?" "That you leave me enough for a first-class, one-way ticket to Palm Beach, and a few years' rent in a deluxe pet hotel, with a standing order for herring and sour cream every morning, and a glass of schnapps every night."

고양이 화장실 속 증조할아버지
(Great-Grandpa's in the Litter Box)

1판 1쇄   2020년 1월 10일
2판 1쇄   2026년 1월 5일

지은이   Dan Greenburg
기획   이수영
책임편집   정소이 박새미
콘텐츠제작및감수   롱테일 교육 연구소
저작권   홍하늘
마케팅   두잉글 사업본부

펴낸이   이수영
펴낸곳   롱테일북스
출판등록   제2015-000191호
주소   04033 서울특별시 마포구 양화로 113, 3층(서교동, 순흥빌딩)
전자메일   help@ltinc.net

ISBN   979-11-93992-34-0   14740

이 도서는 대한민국에서 제작되었습니다.